Scientific Approaches to Goalkeeping in Football

A-Z of Goalkeeping

Andy Elleray

Oakamoor Publishing

Published in 2023 by Oakamoor Publishing, an imprint of Bennion Kearny Limited.

Copyright © Oakamoor Publishing 2023

Andy Elleray has asserted his right under the Copyright, Designs and Patents Act, 1988 to be identified as the author of this book.

ISBN: 978-1-910773-83-3

All Rights Reserved. No part of this publication may be reproduced, stored in a retrieval system, or transmitted in any form or by any means, electronic, mechanical, photocopying, recording or otherwise, without the prior permission of the publisher.

This book is sold subject to the condition that it shall not, by way of trade or otherwise, be lent, re-sold, hired out or otherwise circulated without the publisher's prior consent in any form of binding or cover other than that it which it is published and without a similar condition including this condition being imposed on the subsequent purchaser.

Oakamoor Publishing has endeavoured to provide trademark information about all the companies and products mentioned in this book by the appropriate use of capitals. However, Oakamoor Publishing cannot guarantee the accuracy of this information.

Published by Oakamoor Publishing, Bennion Kearny Ltd
6 Woodside
Churnet View Road
Oakamoor
Staffordshire
ST10 3AE

www.BennionKearny.com

About The Author

Andy Elleray has been working in the goalkeeping world since the age of 16, and playing since the age of seven. His playing career has taken the form of playing at youth academy level and semi-professional level – as well as playing as the sighted goalkeeper for the England and Great Britain Blind Football teams. (Andy also coached the sighted goalkeepers once retiring from playing.)

He has obtained numerous football, academic, and general sporting accolades over the years, including the UEFA A Goalkeeping License, as well as the Advanced Youth Award Goalkeeping License. He also holds a Master's degree in Sports Coaching. All of which have helped shape and evolve goalkeeping practice.

Andy has worked at professional football clubs such as Cheltenham Town, Bristol Rovers, Birmingham City, Liverpool, and Chelsea within different departments in the male game – but with goalkeeping always being at the forefront of his work.

Since 2013, and his first publication, Andy has focused his attention on the female game, working for Birmingham City Women and within the English Football Association's England Talent Pathway as a youth goalkeeping coach. Within this time, he has helped shape some of the brightest goalkeeping talents in the country – helping them to be seen on national and international stages.

During his time at Birmingham, Andy has played a major part in bringing four professional goalkeepers through the ranks, plus 11 goalkeepers representing the home nations at youth international level.

In recent seasons, Andy has coached within the boys Academy at Bristol Rovers FC and within the female Welsh setup as a youth international goalkeeping coach.

This will be Andy's ninth goalkeeping book, all of which will be referenced within this publication and which have been read all over the world.

Andy is keen to pass on his knowledge and expertise to the next generation of budding goalkeeper coaches and goalkeepers. Constantly looking for new and exciting ways in which to evolve the position and cement the position as the most crucial within a football team.

Visit **www.andyelleray.com** for further information on Andy's services, how to get in touch with him, and for other book material.

Introduction

Given my goalkeeping book repertoire, the fact it's taken nearly ten years to produce an A-Z is probably due to the huge amount of depth I've gone into, and the fact there have been so many different research areas within my books.

This publication will be made up of a mixture of characteristics, attributes, roles, playing factors and performance indicators that go into the position of the goalkeeper, with the aim of summarising some of the key elements that make up the goalkeeper.

I'll endeavour to include two to three examples within each letter, most of which will give an overall summary of that particular topic.

Given the snapshot nature of this book, for the real in-depth matter, my other books will elaborate on many of the topics touched upon. Now let's get stuck into an A-Z of goalkeeping!

* Disclaimer – the content and headlines are solely from *my* experiences of key goalkeeping aspects. I accept there will be others along the way that may well make up others' opinions of how goalkeepers should be developed. Or, indeed, what is important!

Agility

When watching goalkeepers in action, at any level, those "worldie" flying saves – where the goalkeeper seems to travel and hang in the air for an eternity – depict what agility looks like in goalkeeping.

The consensus is that agility is defined as the ability to rapidly change direction and react to different stimuli without the loss of balance or body control. This is a requisite of many sports, particularly team and racquet sports. From an injury prevention view, agility helps with muscle activation and helps prevent niggling injuries.

The traditional definition of the ability to change direction rapidly has been redefined, in recent years, as changes of direction and speed; within goalkeeping, this has been pointed out as crucial. This is because of the sport's need for goalkeepers to change direction quickly and frequently, mainly over short distances, and mostly through two different types of agility: planned (or programmed) agility, and reactive (or random) agility.

Goalkeeping research has shown that reactive agility is commonly used as a measure of agility because of the change in stimuli that keepers are faced with in a match.

I'm going to include balance and co-ordination in the agility section, too, as they are very much crucial to agility. Balance is a fundamental for a goalkeeper and involves the maintenance of the body's equilibrium while stationary or moving.

In turn, the ability to stop and change direction cannot be underestimated and builds into many goalkeeping actions. Of course, strength and speed play a big part in balance and coordination, as well as the timing of actions and rhythm. When a top keeper moves, they look aesthetically pleasing and very smooth.

Co-ordination is strongly linked to the biomechanical aspects of goalkeeping. Focusing on footwork and jumping should be attempted, as well as breaking down key elements of an action. Of course, goalkeeping is a position that contains physical contact; by maintaining balance during aerial challenges and even when nudged or bumped, for example, a keeper can remain in a stable position to withstand any physicality and still move.

Training can be slow, at times, when working with younger goalkeepers, but bringing all these components together after movement training is beneficial. Should goalkeepers be gymnasts?! When we look at the above, you could say so!

I want to mention the term *athleticism* here.

Throughout goalkeeping, the term 'athleticism' can be heard a lot of the time. This word, in its original sport-related form, was established in the 19th century in English public schools when referring to physical prowess and athletic sporting game ability. The qualities of athleticism are seen as flexibility, strength, endurance, balance, agility, and explosive coordination.

The National Basketball Association (NBA) in America uses an 'Athleticism Draft Fitness Test' for their incoming crop of potential players. This consists of a series of tests that look at different fitness components such as power, speed, agility, and strength. These tests could be transferable to goalkeeping because of the type of actions they advocate: the initial speed to collect the ball over a short space of time, the ability to jump and beat opponents to the ball, and the ability to change direction quickly in relation to the ball and changes in play, which rely on the goalkeeper to show high levels of athleticism.

Practice

Description

1. The ball starts on the penalty spot with a pre-determined direction of shot.
2. The ball is struck towards this side with the goalkeeper performing a negative step or one-step dive, depending on the distance from their bodyline.
3. The ball must be struck fairly hard due to the fact that the saves in this practice are performed when the goalkeeper doesn't have enough time to move their feet into the ball.

Progressions

1. Make the first strike random.
2. Build in a second phase where the goalkeeper receives a rebound from their first save (if necessary) or a separate second strike from the *same* side that the first ball has been struck.

Main coaching points

- How the goalkeeper deals with the ball – claim or deflect away?
- The goalkeeper's head position on the saves – where is it in relation to the ball?
- Assess where the goalkeeper makes first contact with the ball.
- Try not to act as the server, if possible, as the coach; this way, you can observe the actions more accurately.

Anticipation

A quality such as anticipation is mixed into the decision-making, visual stimuli, and cue recognition domain. But why is anticipation merited in the A-Z? For the goalkeeper, being *ahead of the game* and proactive gives them a fighting chance of responding to what's happening.

Often, the goalkeeper relies on reacting to situations rather than preparing for them; this is the fluid nature of football (of course) in terms of how teams attack. If the goalkeeper can be trained to read cues and triggers – and be in sync with the game – they will be able to respond quicker.

Examples of this would include watching forwards' runs to gauge where and when through passes might be played. Another would be when an opposition player is going to shoot on goal. A third would be their teammates' movement to get on the ball.

All of these moments in the game require the goalkeeper to recognise player movement and ball positioning, which takes high levels of concentration and attention.

From a coaching standpoint, training anticipation requires lots of game-relevant scenarios to train the brain to recognise relevant patterns. Games-based practices are ideal for this as they include appropriate movement patterns and decision-making opportunities in abundance.

The aspiration is to be ahead of the game and stack the odds in the goalkeeper's favour; training to anticipate and predict what they're going to be faced with will allow this to occur.

Barriers To Development

Like any sporting escapade, there are barriers that stop a player from achieving their dreams and reaching their aspirations. The goalkeeper is no exception. This section will cover a selection of common barriers that I've witnessed first-hand during the past 20 years in football.

Focus on the negative and lack of self-belief

I was watching a documentary on an ex-England cricketer this week, and there was a line from a coach about the player that really stuck with me. It was, '*Has anyone ever told him how good he is?*'

This statement is so powerful. Some players don't know how good they actually are, and struggle with believing in themselves.

This reverts back to acknowledging what a player is good at, rather than what they can't do so well. I loathe the term 'weakness' (used so often in recent times) due to its negative connotations. I prefer thinking in a positive tense. For example, I *always* refer to the left and right feet exactly as they are… a left and right foot, not stronger and weaker feet!

Showing keepers what they *can do* using positive visuals such as videos will harness this belief. If, as a coach, you get your language right and make the goalkeeper feel a million dollars, you won't go far wrong.

Overcoming adversity

These could also be known as 'speed bumps' and are occurrences, either planned or not planned, that disrupt and challenge a player's development pathway.

Being able to bounce back from bad games, being drooped, being on the bench, mistakes, or a loss of form for a goalkeeper is important due to the high-pressure nature of the position – and the magnified nature of negative displays.

Having the tools and the strategies to overcome these events (with proper support) will help the player to further their own long-term development and pathway.

Being released

This is probably one of the most extreme moments of adversity a goalkeeper can face – whether that's being released from a club, being told you're not good enough, not gaining a scholarship, or being unsuccessful during a trial period.

These setbacks can lead to a loss of motivation, dropping out of football, and becoming disillusioned with the sport.

Getting the best advice and having a support network around a keeper are crucial. If any of the above circumstances arise, the major task to be done is to seek feedback, evaluate why it's happened, put an improvement plan together, and come back fighting.

Beatable

My own personal reflections over the years – through all the goalkeeping escapades I've been on – lend themselves to the one inevitable notion. Goalkeepers... wait for it... will concede goals.

Every goalkeeper is beatable. Irrespective of age, ability, gender, or creed. It's a fallacy to think that a goalkeeper cannot be beaten. The sooner *the goalkeeper* accepts this, the better. I am not saying they should be happy about this, merely that they need to be realistic.

Many players I've worked with get overly frustrated by conceding goals, and this is harmful within the context of playing well.

The key is to work on and analyse how to avoid soft goals being scored, and how goalkeepers can do the best they can in every circumstance.

This can be done by building in certain objectives within practice. For example, if a practice is tough with regards to the challenge level (the situation could be close to the goal in terms of distance, or there are no defenders to aid the keeper), then expectations and what is deemed 'success' will look different.

In a 1v1 practice, for example, where the goalkeeper is exposed from a through ball, the likelihood that the goalkeeper will be able to save the majority of efforts on goal is slim. So, placing extra emphasis on the ones they do stop is imperative. Another way this can be done is to set targets, such as – in this situation – saving 3 out of 10 repetitions is success for us.

Fallibility is not a weakness, but an expectation. Even the best goalkeepers, over any day and age, have conceded goals, some great ones, and some very bad ones!

Buffon, Gianluigi

A legendary Italian goalkeeper who is still playing at the highest level well into his 40s.

A pioneer in modern goalkeeping, Buffon has achieved everything there is to achieve in football over his illustrious career. He's a true icon of goalkeeping and has inspired a generation of young goalkeepers – none more so than his successor Gianluigi Donnarumma.

What makes him such a good goalkeeper, apart from his physical fitness and motivation, is his 'positional sense'.

How to train like Buffon

- Buffon's game is built on being in the right place at the right time, composure, and assurance. Studying the game by keeping up to speed with the latest tactics and watching the latest matches will help game and role understanding.
- Making notes on top goalkeepers by looking at the *overall* game, not just their shot-stopping, is a really useful way to improve your awareness of the need to read opposition players' movements and how they are looking to play. This will keep you one step ahead and make the game easier by being in the right place at the right time.
- When working with your team in training, narrate to yourself in your own mind what you're seeing and thinking – can I stop this attack by being in this position? What information does that defender need to know? If I was to get the ball, how could I exploit the opposition?
- From a coaching perspective, being exposed to realistic practices aids a goalkeeper's ability to take up the best positions possible to defend the goal, and to defend the area and space in front of them.

Communication

Communication is an interpersonal skill that can have a massive effect on any given situation in football – impacting the feeling and thoughts of the team.

I would class 'communication' as how your message looks/sounds, and information as the specific instructions that are given.

Verbal (oral feedback, instructions, or praise) and visual (a positive or negative gesture, for example) communication dominate the goalkeeper's role. As do actions that show demeanour – such as a player walking away when being spoken to, or not showing some kind of acknowledgement to recognise they've heard or seen a command.

I frequently get asked at youth level: "How can I get my goalkeeper to talk more?" Well, there's no easy answer, although I would say that two things are apparent:

1. Most young keepers don't know what to say.
2. And they don't have the confidence to address their team.

When you're a young goalkeeper, there's so much information to take in, mainly on the technical side, such as focusing on how to physically save the ball and the situation being faced. It goes without saying that the goalkeeper can see the whole picture from their position – so working on communication can keep the team in solid shape and players in the correct positions. Therefore, to start with, focus on getting the goalkeeper to just communicate what they have in their mind at that moment, and not worry a great deal about what information is being given.

Controlling the defence takes game understanding and experience. Giving the goalkeeper appropriate scripted commands, or trigger words, is a good start! Some examples might be:

- 'man on' or 'time'
- 'step up' (followed by distance)
- 'mark' (followed by name)
- 'slide left' or 'slide right' (when the ball moves vertically)

Keepers should also arrange walls and defensive set plays.

All commands should be clear, short, and sharp, using the appropriate tone of voice. Keepers should not commentate; they're not John Motson! If players are monotone and constantly talking, their team will switch off and not respond quickly when they are required to.

Keepers should focus on the players they can directly affect – like organising their defensive shape when the ball is in the attacking third.

As the coach, it's important to show examples of when to use the terms or trigger words, either in training, through video recall, or by watching live games that a player is not involved in. This is why specific game-based exercises and sessions are so important – along with integration into the team.

The second point (they don't have the confidence to address their team) is relevant to the confidence section. Again, it is important for the goalkeeper to integrate with the team to form a relationship and create cohesion with them. I think that once you get the first point (knowing what to say) right, then the second will take care of itself. The thought of saying the wrong thing or 'not knowing your team' can make you very placid. I speak from experience here!

Of course, when wanting to receive the ball, a goalkeeper's commands should be verbal and visual; for example, when wanting to receive the ball on their right foot from a defender: "Right foot John," (showing their right hand at the same time).

Making eye contact with that player is also important, especially when leaving the goalmouth to receive a ball. The defender can see the keeper change position and not look to play the ball where they last saw them, but where they actually are.

Whether verbal or visual, it's crucial in practice sessions that a keeper practices both, and that the goalkeeper understands where and when to use them. The key is to be *loud* and *specific*. Every goalkeeper is different, and personalities will dictate your goalkeeper's type of communication – but once again, giving them the necessary tools and feedback to perform will help a great deal.

Ultimately, the goalkeeper's role in this communication domain is to help their team stop danger. Speaking in a positive tense, when instructing a player what to do, is highly beneficial – an example would be to give information such as 'block ball' or 'press ball' (followed by an individual name). The keeper is telling their teammate what they *want* to happen.

A bad example would consist of 'no shot 'or 'no cross'. The goalkeeper is not actually telling the person receiving the information what they want to happen. The human brain deals in the positive.

Task

As a player, when watching football on television or online, analyse the goalkeeper when they're on screen and put yourselves in their shoes. Look at the play and think about – if you were that player –what information you would give, how you would communicate, and who you would talk to. This practice is useful as you may be faced with the same situation in your games.

Consistency

Delivering consistent performances is essential for any goalkeeper, not just for their own mind, but also to engender trust with the manager or head coach. Consistency, in my experience, is the number 1 reason for selection. If the person in charge of the side can trust and rely on the goalkeeper to perform their basic roles to a high level, and not have a big discrepancy between their 'best and worst', the likelihood of this consistent performer being selected increases dramatically.

Consistency in actions and tactical implementation are crucial as well. If the player goes rogue and off the game plan, this can be highly problematic for a coach. If the player is consistent in their decision-making in possession, then the script can be written with confidence that the goalkeeper will carry out what's asked of them.

An example of this would be where the coach wants to play into the full backs from the goalkeeper, and they can fulfil this in a consistent manner. The successful execution of this type of pass allows the team to be setup in a certain way to build the attack.

Crossing

It's widely accepted in the goalkeeping world that being able to deal with crosses is the hardest thing to master. This is due to the wide range of factors that affect crosses, including the number of players around the ball, a keeper being comfortable with physical contact, weather conditions, and the risk of leaving the goal-line and *not* affecting the ball.

From a coaching perspective, it's important you embrace the challenges when teaching how to deal with crossing. Showing patience, designing realistic practices, and setting expectations (especially in young keepers) that they won't achieve success at every turn – due to the skill's difficulty – are crucial.

Being competent and strong with crosses really sets great goalkeepers apart from the rest. Indeed, it is a manager's dream to have a dominant, commanding, and assured goalkeeper defending their penalty box. It's vital that the goalkeeper portrays an aggressive and imposing stance, showing the opposition they mean business.

Crossing - The Claim

What

The 'claim' is the holy grail for a goalkeeper when crosses rain in. Being able to leave the goal-line and pluck the ball out of the sky offers *no better feeling*, mostly due to the fact (as mentioned) that crossing and aerial play is widely regarded as the toughest goalkeeping skill to master. The claim can take many forms, and this section will go through the most common examples.

When

A claim can occur when the ball is played from a crossed situation. Whether the goalkeeper needs to come through bodies to get to the ball, whether they need to withstand pressure from corners, or if they need to retreat backwards to defend the back post – the same message applies. If you can claim the ball, *then do so*!

Of course, claiming the ball may not be possible due to a number of variables and factors (which will be discussed later in this section), but the need to build confidence and familiarity in claiming crossed balls is vitally important to the demands of the position.

How

The two images show instances when the goalkeeper has to claim the ball (when there is pressure, and when there is a free run to the ball).

Now, there's a case to say that the images are the wrong way around with the protection knee up when there's no pressure (right side), and a two-legged jump (left side). However, the goalkeeper needs to be able to perform *all variations of jump in any situation*. It's important to note that aerial play isn't linear and prescribed, in the sense of 'when this happens, you do this' and 'when that happens, you do that'. Dealing with crossed balls doesn't work in this way! As such, it needs to be trained and developed appropriately.

Training practice

Description

1. The wide player plays the ball in-between the goalkeeper and a central attacking player. The start with the ball and travel into a cutback position.
2. The idea is to give the goalkeeper the opportunity to either intercept the ball or move into a position to react to a close strike on goal.
3. It's important that if the goalkeeper saves the ball, a second phase is played. For example, if the ball is left in the 6-yard box after an initial save, the practice must continue.

Progressions

1. The wide player can take a touch to change the angle of cutback delivery.
2. Add in a second attacker at the back post to increase the situational complexity for the goalkeeper.
3. Build in distribution after the claim, in terms of a counter-attack or longer-range throw/drop kick.
4. Inswinging or outswinging delivery.

Main coaching points

- Make sure the goalkeeper doesn't start in advance of the near post – they will have a great deal of space and distance to cover.
- Is the cutback in an area that the goalkeeper can affect? Either by claiming the ball or deflecting the ball away from the attacking player.
- Observe how they travel across the goalmouth and when/how they set themselves for the strike.
- Allow the goalkeeper to experiment with various saving methods.
- In terms of rebounds, the odds are not in the goalkeeper's favour if the ball is left in the 6-yard box! So, be realistic about where they can deflect or block the ball away to. Easy tap-ins after a great save should still draw praise for the goalkeeper; defenders' help will be needed in these situations!

Crossing - Push Away

What

The push away action is used when dealing with crossed and aerial balls, and it is an amalgamation of the punching techniques. In involves the goalkeeper diverting the ball away from the challenge of an opposing player. Due to the physical nature of crossed balls, there will always be bodies in and around the goalkeeper. So, the opportunity to punch cleanly is not always possible. The push away action gives the goalkeeper an 'out' technique if they've been knocked off balance or misjudged the flight of the ball.

When

This can be used at any time when there is likely to be contact on the goalkeeper. It's an action that allows the goalkeeper, in essence, to 'do what they can' when looking to affect the ball. These instances might include:

When the goalkeeper has been drawn to the ball, realised they have come too far, and now needs to backtrack.

If the goalkeeper sees a teammate near the contact area the goalkeeper will move into.

If the goalkeeper is unable to move their feet and is restricted, maybe from a corner, and being pinned in.

How

The 'how' within this action can look very different, depending on the situation.

There will be times when a full palm contact would be used or a mix of one/two-handed punches.

The goalkeeper in this first image has been caught underneath the ball and is experiencing contact from the attacker. The only way that they can get decent purchase on the ball is to try and push the ball away. They can't use their arms to extend into a punch or manage to get two hands to the ball due to the strong contact from the attacking player.

The second image illustrates the goalkeeper coming around the back of the contact and manging to turn the ball to safety whilst being off balance.

Tactically, once again, when the action has been performed – no matter where or how this is done – the goalkeeper must retreat back to the goal-line due to any second phase that they might need to deal with.

Aside from this section, take a look at 'Punching' in the Ps. Usually, it's an undertaught skill, but one that can be mighty effective. Due to the nature of modern-day footballs – that fly and spin around like crazy – this skill can be used to divert the ball away from danger. If the goalkeeper possesses the ability to punch the ball with decisiveness, they are more confident in their ability to deal with the aerial ball, and hence will *come for more crosses*.

De Gea, David

A Spanish goalkeeper of incredible ability who has played in the Premier League for over a decade. Much criticised in his early days at Manchester United, he has overcome the doubters to become one of the best keepers in recent years.

De Gea's style of goalkeeping relies a great deal on *'Leg/Foot Saves'*, and he combines his high levels of agility and flexibility to perform them on a regular basis. De Gea uses this technique to maximise his effectiveness in making saves. Being 6ft 4 with long limbs makes it hard to get his head and hands down to low balls in and around his body. Being able to use his physical attributes to defend his goal has led him to become one of the best shot-stoppers we've seen in recent times.

Leg saves have been around ever since goalkeeping first appeared. However, it's only in the last decade that they've generally been accepted by the football fraternity as a viable saving action. Many purists want the hands to be the main tool the keeper uses. The acceptance of leg saves stems from the fact that small-sided format techniques (such as Futsal) are permeating mainstream football, and we now see many countries crossing over their approaches from other environments.

There has been a long stigma associated with using leg saves within goalkeeping. Examples include the accusation that leg saves are the 'lazy option'… players just wave their leg at the ball when it's easier and more 'correct' to handle the ball. Either way, the narrative has evolved, and it is now widely accepted that leg saves can play a massive part in the keeper defending the goal… as long as they're used at the right time, in the right way, and to the maximum effect.

How to train like De Gea

Description

1. The key to this practice is the direction and speed of the ball. If the serve is too slow, you'd expect the goalkeeper to either perform a scoop or diving action. If the ball is too far away from the body, then this would bring in a diving save as well. In order to practice leg saves, there will need to be an element of prescribed service, which will lessen the realism. But, as a starting point, this is fine, as the practice can end up being a random shot-stopping practice.

2. The ball is struck towards the goal, through the mannequins, with the goalkeeper working on their leg saves.

Progressions

The circled player is in position for rebounds off the goalkeeper for a second phase action.

Alter the angle and distance of the strikes on goal.

Main coaching points

Factoring in the above analysis of leg saves, in terms of the body position, does the keeper show an intent to get their body through the ball? Lower limb flexibility and the timing of the action are key here.

When practice is random, does the goalkeeper perform the actions the same way, or is there a difference? Differences might include a delay in the decision-making process or physical execution.

Decision Making

A goalkeeper's decision-making in football is crucial due to the ever-changing nature of the environment in front of them. Decisions include where to kick the ball, whether to come and deal with a crossed ball, or what technique to use to catch the ball.

Decision-making can be defined as the process of making a choice between alternatives when the outcome cannot be known in advance. Taking the above example (whether to come and deal with a crossed ball) – the options would be to catch the ball, punch the ball, or leave the ball to be dealt with by the defenders.

Decision-making often involves complex deliberations, such as predicting probable consequences, balancing moral and technical considerations, and attending to the likely impact of the decision on others. No athlete always makes the appropriate decision. This comes down to a number of factors, including experience and muscle memory. A lot of decisions that are made are also tied to emotion.

The process of decision-making is pretty complex! So, without regurgitating a textbook, I will just touch upon the 'phase' system involved.

The perceiving phase – in this phase, the goalkeeper is looking to address the situation and is working out what information is important. So, for example, when considering a cross, decision-making would incorporate the flight of the ball, left-footer or right-footer delivery, defensive and attacking positions, and environmental conditions. With experience, this phase becomes shorter and more autonomous.

The deciding phase – the goalkeeper is now deciding what action to take. Using the above example – shall I come, or stay and catch, or punch?

The acting phase – where the goalkeeper physically carries out the action.

Obviously, all of the above takes place in a fraction of a second. So, it's important players don't overload their minds with lots of questions about the situation they're faced with. As experience increases, they will know how to respond to a whole host of scenarios. In football, no two attacks, saves, or crosses are the same; the decision-making process, however, stays the same. Within practice sessions, incorporate decision-making elements into the exercises (as ability levels increase, a keeper should be able to handle a lot more). The goalkeeper should be allowed to solve problems at every turn.

A clear mind, free from distractions, which enables the athlete to focus solely on the task at hand, is the winning approach. In goalkeeping, you survive due to your decision-making skills.

As a coach, ask your goalkeeper, "What is your thought process when you make this move?" or "What went through your mind when you made this decision?"

Questions like these will invoke an interaction between athlete and coach – potentially to help unclutter the keeper's mind when faced with a split-second decision.

Small hesitations can prove costly, so being positive and sticking to decisions is crucial.

One of the reasons why goalkeepers can carry on playing into their late 30s is because their decision-making processes are grooved, and they can place themselves in appropriate positions despite their inevitable decreasing agility and reaction times; they have been faced with real-life game experiences before and can process situations quickly.

There's no substitute for experience.

Anticipation in goalkeeping is being able to read the game situation and the opposition.

Being in the correct position allows for tough saves to become easier and for players to be one step ahead of the opposition. Anticipation in goalkeeping has been researched in the last few years. Results have found that total gaze fixation time and average gaze fixation time were longer when a kick was anticipated successfully. Also, information obtained through the peripheral vision system (while fixing one's gaze on an optic clue) was deemed the most important element behind successful anticipation.

One particular study found that with penalty kicks – expert goalkeepers were generally more accurate in predicting the direction of the penalty kick and waited longer before initiating a response. They also found that expert goalkeepers used a more efficient search strategy involving fewer fixations – of longer duration – to less disparate areas of the display. The novices spent longer fixating on the trunk, arms, and hips, whereas the experts found the kicking leg, non-kicking leg, and ball areas to be more informative, particularly as the moment of foot-to-ball contact approached.

In essence, expert goalkeepers reduce the amount of information to be processed by using their peripheral vision to a greater effect. Expert goalkeepers can anticipate where the ball is going and what their next actions must be; for example, telling their defence to shift left or right, or positioning themselves in an appropriate position in the goal area to save a shot.

Petr Cech used different techniques to improve his peripheral vision during his career. One utilised a screen that contained 500 lights, and he had to hit the appropriate light as soon as it illuminated. Another was a machine that fired out different coloured balls at varying angles and speeds. As Christophe Lollichon explained, "You mustn't move your head but only your eyes, as that's how to improve your peripheral vision, which is essential as a goalkeeper has to spot dangers coming from all sides." Although this type of equipment is only available to those at the top level, it's certainly interesting to see how goalkeepers are looking to prepare and train in the modern era. Further into this book, the vision and awareness section will examine this more.

If you are a coach, your training environment must replicate the situations your goalkeepers are faced with on a match day.

Without harping on about the benefits of varied decision-making-based practices, it is worth stating that these environments breed a goalkeeper that can respond to whatever they face in a match. Specific match-based practices, team tactical play, or tailored game practices are the way forward here.

We must arm our goalkeepers with the tools needed to fight the opposition; to respond to every type of shot from every type of distance. From giving them numerous ways in which to distribute effectively to the defensive, midfield, and attacking thirds, to showing them different set plays they will be exposed to and how to handle subtle changes of movement from the opposition.

Is playing out to my left back the right pass? How can I distribute early down the field? What is the best option now to build an attack? The game changes so fast that the movement of one player can change the picture the goalkeeper sees.

Decision-making is arguably the most important element for a goalkeeper; the good news is that this is something that can be taught via realistic training drills. An exercise as simple as playing a variety of different through balls with someone bearing down on goal, and leaving the keeper with the decision to come and collect or hold their ground is highly beneficial.

Similar drills for crossing can also be useful. They need not be too complicated, provided they are realistic and test the goalkeeper in this specific area. Linked to this is the mental aspect; bad decisions will often come from a cluttered mind.

Practices

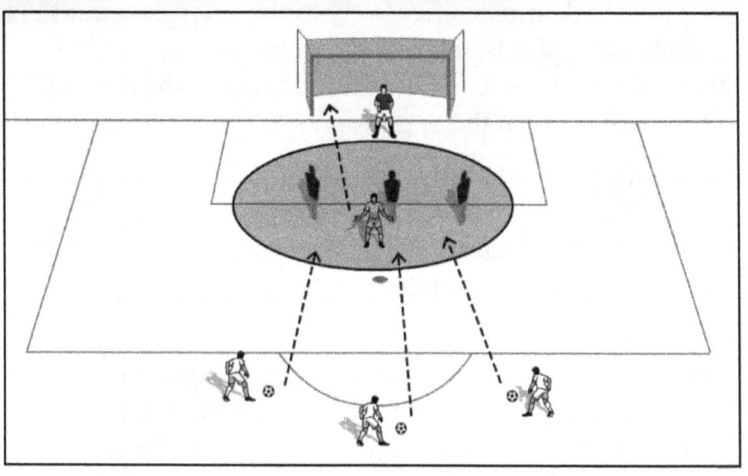

Description

1. A server starts on the penalty spot, and can receive the ball from a teammate from any angle outside the penalty area.
2. They can strike on goal first or second time, trying to score.
3. The goalkeeper's focus is on deflecting the ball away, so the attacker doesn't have a second strike on goal.

Progressions

1. Allow the attacker to finish any loose balls.
2. Move the attacker's starting point in line with either post to bring in some new strike angles.

Main coaching points

- The goalkeeper will need to limit their movement due to the proximity of the attacker.
- Identify how quickly the goalkeeper is able to transfer their weight through the ball when they're not looking to secure it.

- The goalkeeper must return to their feet as quickly as possible after they perform the save.

Description

1. The key to this practice is the direction and speed of the ball. If the serve is too slow, you'd expect the goalkeeper to either perform a scoop or diving action. If the ball is too far away from the body, then this would bring in a diving save as well. In order to practise leg saves, there will need to be an element of prescribed service, which will lessen the realism. But, as a starting point, this is fine as the practice can end up being a random shot-stopping practice.
2. The ball is struck towards goal through the mannequins, with the goalkeeper working on their leg saves.

Progressions

The circled player is in position for rebounds off the goalkeeper for a second phase action.

Alter the angle and distance of the strikes on goal.

Main coaching points

- Factoring in the above analysis of leg saves, in terms of body position, does the keeper show an intent to get their body through the ball? Lower limb flexibility and the timing of the action are key here.
- When practice is random, does the goalkeeper perform the actions the same way, or is there a difference? Differences might include a delay in the decision-making process or physical execution.

Diving

When someone thinks of a goalkeeper, one of the main images that get conjured up is of a player who is flying through the air, outstretched arm, trying desperately to reach the football.

But why does a goalkeeper need to dive? It's usually when attempting to save the ball away from their bodyline; a last option as once they perform a dive, there's no reversing this movement – unless they've discovered the Matrix!

There are a variety of dive types that a goalkeeper can perform, such as a high dive, mid-height dive, low dive, negative step dive, and step and dive. All of which have their own time to be used and methods of execution.

From a biomechanical view, every goalkeeper will dive differently. The need to make this safe is paramount due to the high levels of effort and force involved, plus landing (at times) from a great height.

There are loads of examples and in-depth analyses of diving action in my 'Basics' book.

Practice

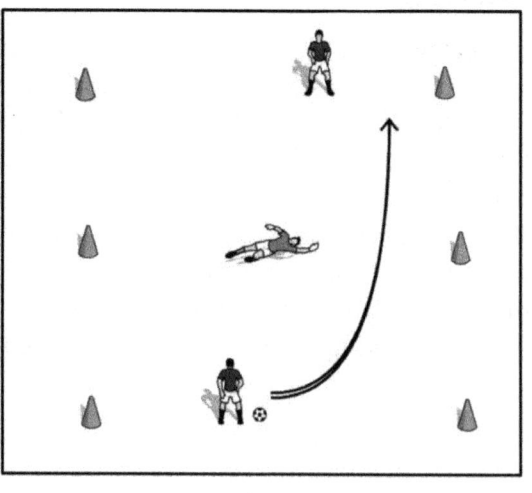

Explanation

The goalkeeper at each end must get the ball over to the goalkeeper at the opposite end, using one method of distribution at a time. For example, it could be ground kicking a stationary ball, throwing, or a moving ball where a lay-off is provided by the goalkeeper in the middle. The goalkeeper in the middle will have a designated area to stay in.

The goalkeeper in the middle will try to stop the ball; if they succeed, they will get one point. If the goalkeeper at either end gets the ball over to the opposite side, this is again worth one point.

The winner will be the goalkeeper with the most points once everyone has been in each position. For progressions, you could change the position of the middle goalkeeper's area, plus increase or decrease the size of the grid.

Starting positions
- Coach plays the ball into either end player
- The goalkeeper in the middle starts with the ball, plays to either end player (underarm roll or pass), and has to react off their first touch

Ederson

The Brazilian goalkeeper Ederson embodies the modern-day requirement to be excellent with the ball at one's feet; he is composed on the ball and shows great passing capabilities to build attacks from the back.

His 'ball playing ability' was born playing as an outfield player, and he participated in a variation of Futsal whilst growing up in Brazil. His left foot has proven to be a real weapon for his national team, and of course, his club side – Manchester City – where he is a crucial part of how the team plays.

How to train like Ederson

Being a goalkeeper, it's tempting to just go in goal and take shots day after day after day.

But if you want to really stand out, being able to use the ball at your feet will make you a much more complete player – and increase your chances of playing a big part within a team.

Simple practices such as grabbing a bag of balls and looking to hit targets all over the pitch are valuable. Being part of a team's passing and possession practices will also aid the development of playing under pressure and general receiving skills.

From an outfield perspective, 'Ball Mastery' is the practice of technical routines in a tight amount of space which allows individuals to get literally hundreds of touches on the ball in a short amount of time. The practice challenges players to control and manipulate the ball with the different surfaces of their feet. This can take the form of ball manipulation, dribbling, running with the ball, shielding and turning, and body feints.

For goalkeeping, of course, the above is very useful. The way I'd frame mastering the ball for a goalkeeper is getting the ball to do what you want it to do. This means the following:

- Being able to put speed, spin, curve, drift and drop upon the football. Using a golf club analogy, the goalkeeper needs more than one way to pass the ball. And where possible, with BOTH feet.

- Having an assured first contact on the ball, which allows them time and/or space to then select the best possible pass available.
- Being comfortable with playing first time and under pressure from the opposition.

Education (for coaches)

Goalkeeping coach education all around the world has progressed a great deal in the past ten years. The opportunity to take specific courses, delivered by experienced and expert tutors has accelerated the sharing of knowledge around the position in all areas, from the physical to the psychological.

Looking at the English FA, they offer Levels 1 and 2, which cover the basics and fundamentals of the position, then the UEFA B and A courses, which delve into the tactical and holistic development of the goalkeeper a coach works with.

To complement this, there is an Advanced Youth Award in coaching goalkeepers, which looks at the age and playing level, specifically, of being a modern-day goalkeeper.

Having been through the A License and the Advanced Youth Award myself, the opportunity to dissect not only the position, but the role a goalkeeper coach can play, has been valuable.

The overriding feeling is that by addressing the development of more than just the technical side of the position (which used to be the case), coaches all over the world improve the standard of goalkeeper coaching for everyone.

The big debate amongst the goalkeeping fraternity is the prerequisite to complete outfield coaching badges *before* being allowed to enrol on goalkeeping-specific courses. The importance of understanding the game as a whole is important for coaches, which makes this stance logical and – for me – the right approach.

Wherever you are in the world, contact your local and national Football Associations for information on courses that are offered. Take every opportunity to increase your knowledge of goalkeeping!

Energetic

ENERGY! I think this needs to be included as – without this quality – it's very hard for a player to develop and reach their potential or performance goals.

Goalkeeping can be physically and mentally tough. Having the mindset to give maximum energy day in, day out, separates the good from the great.

The enthusiasm needed to train on a cold, wet Thursday morning in early December is never easy.

The *joy of goalkeeping* section (to come) will elaborate on some of these points, but ask yourself, is *your* energy infectious?

Evolution

For those of us who are avid football fans, the evolution of the roles and responsibilities of the goalkeeper is clear to see. From standing in the goal waiting for involvement, to now receiving the ball near the halfway line, the position has probably seen the most changes compared to any other position on the pitch (with maybe the exception of the modern full-backs, who are now serial assistors; Trent Alexander-Arnold and Andy Robertson being notable examples).

Ever since association football's official organisation date in 1863, the role has – of course – seen changes. From the creation of the penalty area and the back pass law, to tactical integration from teams such as the 2008-2012 Barcelona team under Pep Guardiola and the Bayern Munich teams featuring the great Manuel Neuer. The position experiences fashions, fads, and phases.

In recent times, presence and height have proven to be standout physical features. Tactically, the sweeper-keeper, the ball-playing keeper, and the intelligent keeper who picks passes, is tactically adaptable, and can command the penalty area, have come to the fore.

Who knows what the next chapter of the goalkeeper has in store? The role reflects and moulds to the demands of the game, but one thing is clear – a goalkeeper will always be tasked with keeping the ball out of the net!

Foot/leg Saves

A favourite area of mine, and one that divides opinion amongst the football fraternity. Foot and leg saves are great skills that have become more commonly used by goalkeepers in mainstream football. The influence of formats such as Futsal and a merging of different cultural methodologies has led to the appearance of different save types in the past 10-15 years. Leg and foot saves are no exception.

Although these saves have been around ever since goalkeeping first appeared, it has only been in the last decade that they've generally been accepted by the football fraternity as a viable saving action. Many purists want the hands to be the main tool the keeper uses.

There has long been a stigma associated with using leg saves within goalkeeping. Examples include the accusation that leg saves are the 'lazy option'... players just wave their leg at the ball when it's easier and more 'correct' to handle the ball. Either way, the narrative has evolved, and it is now widely accepted that leg saves can play a massive part in the keeper defending the goal, as long as they're used at the right time, in the right way, and to maximum effect.

These types of saves require a large amount of lower leg dexterity and continual practice to groove them. I would wholeheartedly recommend making foot saves a part of every goalkeeping programme. For an in-depth look at these saves and different variations of them, please see my 'Goalkeeping Basics' book.

Practice

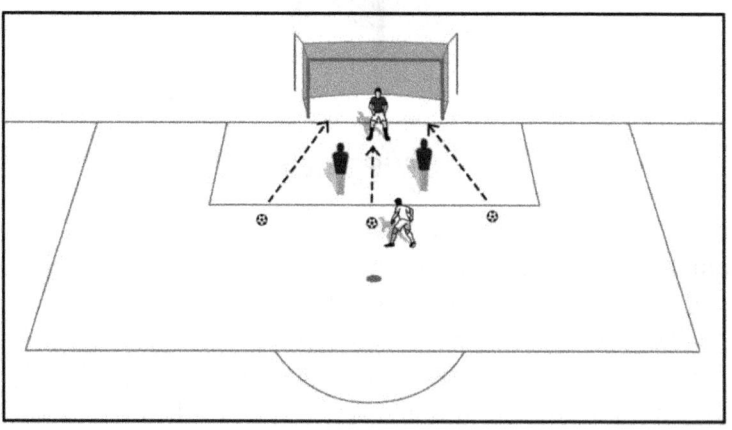

Description

1. The key to this practice is the direction and speed on the ball. If the serve is too slow, you'd expect the goalkeeper to either perform a scoop or diving action. If the ball is too far away from the body, then this would bring in a diving save as well. In order to practice leg saves, there will need to be an element of prescribed service, which will lessen the realism. However, as a starting point, this is fine as the practice can end up being a random shot-stopping practice.
2. The ball is struck towards goal through the mannequins, with the goalkeeper working on their leg saves.

Progressions

The circled player is in position for rebounds off the goalkeeper for a second phase action.

Alter the angle and distance of the strikes on goal.

Main coaching points

In terms of body position, does the keeper show an intent to get their body through the ball? Lower limb flexibility and the timing of the action are key here.

When practice is random, does the goalkeeper perform the actions the same way, or is there a difference? Differences might include a delay in the decision-making process or physical execution.

Footballs

The goalkeeper is always the innocent victim of the advancing technology that goes into the construction of the footballs we currently use. The dip, swerve, pace, and general unpredictability of the balls make it increasingly tougher to save.

The ability to pick up these variants and assess the ball becomes more complex because of their irregular nature. As such, the reaction time is reduced for selecting how to save or approach the ball; without a doubt, this makes the job more difficult.

I'm sure readers who have played in the position will recall stories of late ball movement, using a ball for the first time, being helpless from 35 yards, and seeing a crazy amount of spin placed upon the ball.

An account from my own playing days is when I caught a ball on the end of my finger, causing lots of swelling – I still bear the results of this today! Another famous account is the Brazilian wing-back Roberto Carlos sending a free kick against France around the opposite side of the ball and curving it back violently into the net. So much curve was put on the ball, a ball boy stationed to that side of the goal thought it was coming directly at him… until it spun back to give Carlos another goal to add to his tally. What hope do we have of saving that?!

The last 20 years have seen the most innovation in developing footballs, with some iconic ones such as the Adidas Jabulani and the latest Nike Aerowsculpt. What the manufacturing and aerodynamical minds have in store next will be interesting to see.

The number of companies making footballs has also increased; most competitions in England, at least, use a different ball manufacturer. Hence, before each competition, teams need to work with the tournament ball in order to become familiar with it. For a goalkeeper, new ball challenges can be mixed, but the need to become accustomed to a new ball – *before match days* – is vital.

GK Union

The Goalkeeper's Union! A group where many wish to operate and understand the inner workings of these likeminded individuals. In folklore, the Goalkeeper's Union is a term that is used to describe the goalkeeping life; unless you are (or have been) a goalkeeper, it's virtually impossible to understand and empathise with what the goalkeeper goes through, both on and off the pitch.

Many an anecdote has been attributed to the GK Union, such as the overprotection of goalkeepers from other goalkeepers, goalkeeping coaches never blaming their player for anything, and strong camaraderie (regardless of the circumstance) by those in the union.

There is a wonderful romance in a group of people working together, challenging each other, and putting across the same passion day in, day out, I think.

The union is strong. All over the world, in every country, there are likeminded people immersed in goalkeeper training and chatter. To become a fully-fledged member, you subscribe to all the idiosyncrasies around the position, such as an obsession with gloves, an enjoyment of volleys, and an acceptance you'll make the odd crazy blunder every now and again!

Gloves

Every goalkeeper's vice! As I write, there are hundreds of different gloves available. The most common question I get asked by parents is, 'what gloves are best?'. It's a very tough question to answer, in all fairness, due to the number of factors involved.

Age, gender, playing experience, physical maturation, comfort, hand size, and wrist circumference. Of course, most of these change over time and glove preferences will shift accordingly.

Gloves predominantly started appearing on the football pitch in the 1970s. Cloth gloves were the first, and they have evolved into what we see today. There are a couple of books written on the history of gloves that are out there, if you are interested.

Why goalkeepers use gloves can be looked at from a grip and protection viewpoint. Purchase on the ball is fundamental to securing and manipulating the ball, depending on the circumstances. Protection takes the form of guarding the hands and wrist from excess force. Footballs can swirl and dip all over the place and the likelihood of catching a finger at the wrong angle can lead to much distress (looking at the state of my hands, I should know!).

In principle, not becoming over-reliant on the gloves to do the basic work of contacting the ball is paramount.

Glove manufacturers have created numerous types of 'cut' which cater for different types of hand sizes. These cuts are ever-evolving. Examples would be negative, roll-finger, hybrid, and extension.

Let me explain these further:

Negative: A flat catching surface, internally (negatively) stitched with latex gussets. This style of glove is perfect for the goalkeeper who likes a tighter fit and more feel on the ball. The thumbs of the negative cut gloves are negatively stitched on the underside (unless double-wrapped with latex), providing a tighter, more streamlined feel of the glove.

Roll finger: The latex on this cut wraps/rolls all the way around the fingers from back to front. This creates the maximum latex-to-ball contact, providing great catching security. A roll finger goalkeeper glove creates a more substantial feel on the hands, in comparison with a negative cut or hybrid style.

Hybrid: This glove cut combines the best features of both roll finger and positive cut glove styles – which is why it is referred to as a hybrid cut.

The middle two fingers are positively or negatively (depending on glove model) stitched in a catch-ready position. The outside (index and pinky) fingers are semi-rolled at the top, providing more latex-to-ball contact and catching security.

Extension: provides extra reach and extra margin for that game-changing save. The engineered fit sets hands in a catch-ready position with exceptional hand-to-ball coverage

These different types of gloves allow the goalkeeper to use gloves in different conditions and on different surfaces.

There are now different types of sprays that enhance the grip on glove latex, too. They allow gloves to last longer by being able to wash the gloves more thoroughly; a parent's dream as they don't need to go purchase new pairs as regularly!

Lots of players like to match their gloves with their boots in terms of styles, designs, and colours. This has become a crucial part of the aesthetics and image of the position. To the detriment of performance? Possibly.

Task

Look at the gloves you wear and check if they are the right size and fit your hands well. Many keepers don't wear gloves that either fit or suit their hand shape, which inhibits their ability to get a good feel on the ball.

Whatever brand you use or indeed prefer, don't be afraid to try new styles or manufacturers in the quest of finding the ultimate glove for you.

Height

In all of my previous publications, I've not directly referenced height, and this is a deliberate ploy. It's science fact that you can't control how tall someone is going to be. You can predict through bone scanning, predict through family genetics, and create an environment to be healthy, but you can't 'make' somebody taller.

Height can be a really contentious issue within the world of goalkeeping. Indeed, on platforms such as LinkedIn, players searching for a club sometimes put their height directly after their name to draw attention to it!

Individuals, clubs, and organisations often have a preconceived idea about a minimum height being a pre-requisite to becoming a capable goalkeeper. Being 6ft 4+

automatically gives a keeper some kind of superpower, they feel. I'm being glib, of course, but the obsession over height and making height a big part of the conversation can be damaging. Often, very talented goalkeepers are overlooked because they don't fit a perceived physical profile.

Height has its advantages when it comes to certain situations, of course, but in my opinion, to rule a player in or out solely based on how tall they are (or will be in the future) is risky – there's so much more to coaching and development than this.

Heroic

Any good plot needs a good hero or heroine. The goalkeeper can provide this with penalty saves to win shootouts, worldie flying saves to retain a lead for their side, or by even scoring when coming up from a last-ditch corner kick.

With the trepidation that the role produces, when these moments of being the winning component come along, they should be celebrated with gusto!

Moments in history such as Jimmy Glass's last-gasp goal to keep Carlisle in the football league, Sergio Goycochea's penalty saving in the 1990 World Cup for Argentina, or David de Gea's 14 save colossus vs Arsenal in 2018 are iconic moments.

Fearlessness and courage are relatable qualities that are needed to play the role of the hero or heroine. A good way of putting it is that the goalkeeper needs to *seize the moment* to be heroic and to write their name in legend. They must step up, when required, when all hope seems lost, and are needed to pull a rabbit from the hat.

I

Injuries

Injuries are part and parcel of contact sports, and football is no exception. Goalkeeping is a role that requires high levels of robustness and being able to withstand physical challenges.

Very rarely, probably starting from 16/17 years old, a goalkeeper will always be playing with small knocks and niggles. In part, this is due to the fact that physical training sessions are often harder and more demanding than actual matches themselves.

Having an awareness of the physicality of goalkeeping, from both contact and non-contact injuries is massively important, so you know what you're in store for.

Indeed, a common trait for young players wanting to go in goal is a 'no fear' attitude of getting their head in, and throwing themselves all over the ground.

Common injuries that I see:

Finger injuries

Common to every goalkeeper. Look at a retired professional and their hands usually resemble a Picasso painting!

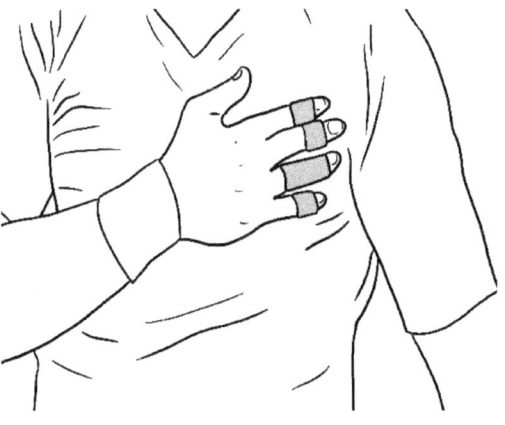

Injuries to fingers are among the most common ways soccer goalies get hurt. The most frequent injury happens when the ball hits the fingers and forces them to jam or bend incorrectly. Fingers might also be stepped on, smashed by another player, or slammed into the goal post.

The best way for goalies to protect themselves from future injuries is to tape their fingers and wear gloves to protect them. In addition, incorporating goalkeeper-specific exercises with a medicine ball, as well as throwing and catching drills, will strengthen fingers and hands.

Also, playing with age-appropriate balls and having older players exercise caution when shooting at younger goalkeepers can help reduce hand injuries and radius fractures in practice.

Wrist injuries

Fractures to the radius bone can happen when the hand is driven backwards towards the wrist. This happens most often when trying to make a save from a direct shot. Radius bone fractures are commonly seen in adolescent goalkeepers.

Strapping the wrists is now common practice for goalkeepers to provide more stability. Given the high volume of hand contacts during a common week, this helps to absorb the shock from balls struck at them. Also, wrist supports can be used at certain times.

Knocks to the head

Putting your head in where it hurts is a big risk – the highest profile example being Petr Cech's incident where he was struck with the trailing leg of Reading forward Stephen Hunt. The consequences of this led Cech to wear a specially-designed skull cap in order to prevent further damage to his head.

I've been kicked in the head, the mouth, and run into; they all hurt. Through balls and corners make the goalkeeper a prime candidate to be 'roughed' up a bit. It's important that when the goalkeeper is lowering their head to smother or engage with the ball, that they tuck their head in to avoid any contact.

It should be pointed out, however, that the protection of goalkeepers is a lot better these days than it used to be; much like the sport as a whole.

Leg muscle strains

Muscle strains can occur in a variety of body parts, from the back to the glutes to the legs. The hamstring is probably the muscle that is most often strained. Goalkeepers need to jump, dive, and move in a number of ways to stop shots. Goalkeepers can also endure a leg injury by kicking the ball down the pitch. One of the most common ways that goalkeepers suffer muscle strain in modern football is due to rushing out of goal to cover for defenders.

Ways to avoid overuse injuries and strains are to warm up and cool down effectively – especially during puberty. In turn, as players begin to train more often, recovery strategies are vital. These should include stretching programmes and ice baths.

As I write this section, I look at my bent index finger and the previously dislocated ring finger on my left hand! All part of the position, I guess…

Intelligence

The old perception that you must be crazy to be a goalkeeper does ring true in some respects. What right-minded person would stick their head into a melee of feet, come through bodies to punch a ball, or be subjected to relentless diving repetitions on an Astroturf floor? What do all these examples have in common, though? They are all linked to the physical side of goalkeeping…

Whilst the thrust of any 'crazy' label is that someone is reckless and not in their right mind, the exact opposite must be the case for any goalkeeper who wants to fulfil the position to a good level. And of the many factors underpinning success, I think calmness is critical for clear thinking. Remaining calm and composed will help the goalkeeper make better decisions more often than not.

Inter-Connected

There are many reasons why the old 'Keeper's Corners' analogy is very much outdated. It's the space where keepers go to train – away from the team at any given moment – doing their own thing and playing by their own rules. The goalkeeper is a vital way for teams to play in terms of building attacks and defending the space behind the defence – in that sense, they need to be part of training practices that work on positioning, defending the area, and staying connected to the team.

The need to communicate and build relationships with the team cannot be done in isolated practice settings and needs to be grooved when working with the team – on and off the pitch. This means that many of my current training environments are weighted more towards training with the team on the pitch, with *specific goalkeeper training* taking place before (or in the early part) of a session.

The majority of the skills and game awareness that the goalkeeper needs to possess can be developed through effective coaching in team practices – some examples of which will be explored in the next sections. Many specific cues and triggers that come with saving shots, engaging crosses, and starting the attack from different points can only be worked upon *effectively* when there are players from both teams; the relevant distances and pitch location, and any external tempo, can only be created by actual match play.

The key – when a goalkeeper is working with the team, whether a goalkeeper coach is present or not – is to set realistic objectives and targets to focus on. Without generalising, the goalkeeper is often not catered for (or planned for) in a session; they are just either 'in the goal' or 'an end player to recycle the ball', which is a simplistic and neglectful viewpoint.

Task

Within your football environment, write down how much time the goalkeepers spend with the team and how much time they spend in goalkeeping sessions in a week. See what the ratio is and if you're hitting what you want. This could be logged for a whole month and an analysis conducted on how the goalkeepers are used within all training sessions.

Joys of Goalkeeping

In order to love the position, you have to love everything that comes with goalkeeping. The joy of throwing yourself in the mud to save a firmly-placed shot into the bottom corner must have a place next to letting a ball through your legs in the last minute of a game to lose 1-0. They're both inextricably linked. The joy doesn't come from the second act, of course, but to experience joy in the first, you must accept that the second is an inseparable part of the role – so enjoy the good moments when you can.

Building the joy of being a goalkeeper usually stems from what I call a 'catalyst moment'. Diving in the mud, stopping a really tough shot, getting pushed into goal because no one wants to do it, replacing an injured player or getting cheers from the parents who are watching when you do something good. All of these are catalyst moments I've seen and are all valid in equal measure.

The key is welcoming and keeping that joy, and embracing the fundamental reasons that you started playing in the position. It's easy to be deterred after bad games or bad sessions, but no matter how serious the game gets, *keep the joy* – it will stand you in good stead, in both good and bad times! I suppose that I must find joy in writing; this is my ninth book on goalkeeping!

Jump Mechanics

Imagine being able to jump like a basketball or volleyball player whilst keeping goal. Well, with the right type of training, this is entirely feasible.

Plyometrics seeks to enhance explosive reactions through powerful muscular contractions due to rapid eccentric contractions, allowing muscles to exert maximum force in the shortest amount of time possible, which – for the reactive and intuitive goalkeeper – is important.

For the muscles to respond explosively, the eccentric contraction is then quickly switched to the isometric (when the downward movement stops) and then the concentric contraction in a minimum amount of time. This allows the goalkeeper to jump upwards as high as possible.

Plyometrics have been found to have benefits for lower extremity injury prevention, as well.

Plyometric exercises should focus on quality not quantity and performed at 95-100% effort. Recovery is important here; a general rule of thumb is to allow 1-3 minutes recovery between sets, and 3-5 minutes between exercises in a training session.

Ultimately, increasing both *speed* and *power* are the key goals of plyometrics. Jumping and landing is another huge area, specific to the role of a keeper. At a young age, jumping and landing should all be about control, movement quality, and stability. Developing the ability to jump dynamically, but with good execution, is essential before moving on to maximal jumping exercises.

Plyometric training can be an important tool for developing explosive power in goalkeepers, but you put the player at serious risk if their basic jumping and landing control is poor. This control ties in with squatting and single-leg squat variations massively. If you watch the take-off and landing phases at the top level, the impact forces and loading that go through the lower extremities (when a keeper dives and jumps) are huge.

Therefore, movement *quality* needs to be of a high level to reduce the risk of potential injury. Working with many young athletes (and in some cases older athletes), the ability to sub-maximally jump (and land) is really quite poor, and those with poor squat, single leg squat, and lunging movement patterns are usually the ones with poor jumping and landing competency. It again reinforces the importance of these fundamental movement and athletic competency exercises for long-term development.

Practice

Description

1. The practice will give the goalkeeper the opportunity to work on various different jump types (one- and two- footed).
2. The ball is played into the penalty area with an attacker trying to get on the end of the cross.
3. The goalkeeper looks to affect the ball.

Progressions

1. Add in another attacker and/or defender to increase complexity.
2. Change the crossing range to give the goalkeeper different ball flights and entries.

3. Inswinging or outswinging deliveries.

Main coaching points

- How early is the goalkeeper able to assess the ball?
- What does hand contact look like, in terms of timing, and the amount of purchase the keeper gets on the ball?
- How does the goalkeeper deal with contact and being off balance?
- If the ball is way out of the goalkeeper's reach, make sure they drop off into the line of contact to prepare for a save.

Kicking

Kicking was something I definitely struggled with at an early age. This was partly due to the fact I only ever played in goal, and I was never taught how to actually kick a ball. It sounds funny, I know, but like any technique, it has to originate from somewhere and be honed through guided discovery, feedback, and instruction.

Biomechanically and physically, there are lots of elements that affect a player's ability to kick a ball. These include hip flexibility/stability, balance/proprioception, lower limb strength, and ankle function. A common issue with goalkeepers around the ages of 12-15 is that physical maturation is changing, and many of the elements mentioned above suffer or alter due to puberty.

'Bambi on Ice' is a coined term for a player who lacks the control and understanding of their body! If you have ever seen a baby deer struggling to stand up, you will know what I mean.

During this period of development, goalkeepers will struggle with power, range, and accuracy of kicking. Outfield coaches wishing to build a certain tactical strategy that includes their goalkeepers must be aware of this. As pitch sizes increase with this age range of youth development, goalkeepers can become frustrated around the fact they can't play over longer distances. There's nothing wrong with this. With the correct support, acceptance, and understanding around the player, their ability to develop physically, and then technically, will eventually come.

Kicking a football in terms of putting 'detail' or 'texture' on the ball relies on the player consciously deciding how they want the ball to get to its intended destination. This would include backspin, curve, driving the ball, and lofting the ball. Different situations require different methods of ball distribution and 'contact' upon the ball.

I guess the overriding message is not to assume the goalkeeper knows how to kick the ball. Like anything football-related, it needs to be worked on.

Practice

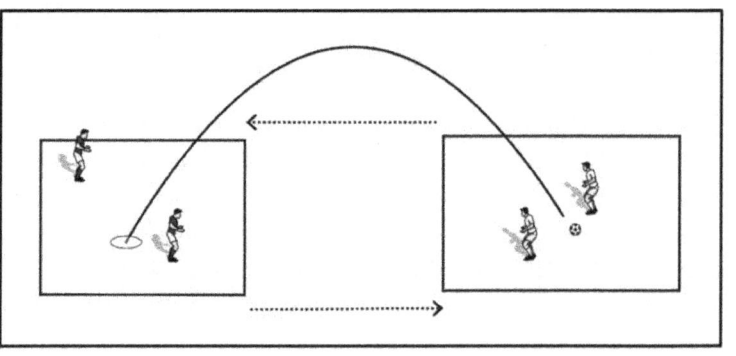

Explanation

The aim of the game is to avoid the ball bouncing in your zone. The team in control of the ball will aim for the opponent's zone (marked out by cones) using an agreed method of distribution. This could be throwing, drop kicks, stationary goal kicks, or moving back passes. If the ball does bounce inside a team's area, the opponents will receive a point and vice-versa. If a ball fails to reach the zone or goes out of play, the ball will go to the other team.

When a goalkeeper gains control, they must distribute the ball within six seconds if it's in their hands. They can gain control by catching the ball directly or controlling it with their body (to replicate a back pass). Try to use one at any time, not both. Keep the game realistic by encouraging goalkeepers to play quickly.

The example grid can be changed according to the session topic, or a diagonal game can be created to work on distribution into wide areas.

Game starting positions

- One of the teams starts with the ball.
- The coach plays the ball to one of the teams from a varied position.
- The coach plays the ball in.

Kit

The goalkeeper always stands out on the football pitch because they wear different attire to the other players. Indeed, some people are attracted to the position due to the uniqueness of the playing shirt and the exclusive role! This tells us something about the types of personalities that are attracted to the position. Ones that enjoy standing out, who thrive on the responsibility to protect and defend something, and who are (at times) isolated from the main group of people. The psychology and dynamic behind this would make for a great book in itself.

Goalkeepers in football, in its modern and relatable format, have always worn a different kit. The patterns, colours, and varieties of these go down in folklore. From Jorge Campos's florescent Mexican kit to the crazy patterns in the Premiership during the mid-90s, and not excluding Jose Luis Chilavert's lion-based shirt (which fitted his personality perfectly), these kits are as iconic as the people who wore them.

Last Line of Defence

There is something poetic about the goalkeeper being the last line of defence. Where every other player has failed or been sacrificed, the goalkeeper is the final hope for the team!

The goalkeeper has been described as the 'jewel in the crown' and that allowing the ball to get to them is sacrilege; the team must fight tooth and nail for this not to happen, or more plainly, defend well.

It is important that the goalkeeper embraces this sentiment and not feel (or take) sole responsibility for conceding a goal. Even soft goalkeeping errors should, at times, have been prevented before their involvement.

As the last line of defence, the goalkeeper is – by definition – the first line of attack, and that's a narrative played out throughout this book.

Long-Term Development

It's been said that male goalkeepers don't reach their 'peak' until their early to mid-30s, and females slightly before, in their late-20s. There are, of course, exceptions to the rule.

With this in mind, experience and knowing one's game are key parts of reaching peak potential, whatever that might be.

It takes years to develop the necessary skill set to be an all-round, top-class goalkeeper. This lengthy path of development needs to have a bearing on the long-term development of young goalkeepers such that coaches show patience when individuals are learning how to play the position. This means that during the foundation years, people must not expect the player to be mini-Jordan Pickfords or Ellie Roebucks. They need to build up their technical consistency, physical capability, psychological robustness, and tactical nous through session upon session of deliberate practice. I call this the 'goalkeeping years', which indicates how long the player has played the position for, and what kind of experiences they have.

The nature of youth development is that each player develops at a different rate and in different ways. Some individuals may pick up the attributes required to be a goalkeeper quicker than others or be born with them… (we won't get into a nature vs nurture debate here!).

From a physical perspective, work completed at younger ages can potentially shape an athlete's or goalkeeper's career. Often people talk about models of Long-Term Athletic Development (LTAD) and relate this to physical, social, technical, and psychological progressions.

The LTAD should be about three main things:
1. Quality Education
2. Appropriate Content
3. Justifiable Progression

It is certainly not a set-in-stone process as each athlete/goalkeeper is different and will therefore progress differently.

Often coaches, sport scientists and other people who have contact with young sportspeople get them to do drills, exercises, or work which are detrimental to that individual's development. Often, it is because a player – at that time – is too physically or technically weak to complete the task.

In many cases, a lack of coach awareness underpins why someone is doing a certain drill/exercise. Examples might be gym-based weight training or high-intensity speed drills.

This highlights the importance and duty we have, as coaches, to understand our area of expertise thoroughly and show a willingness to be educated and develop. In doing so, our practices will too.

Goalkeeping at the highest level involves big multi-joint powerful movements from jumps to sprints, catching to throwing, all of which are multi-directional and done at high speed in an explosive nature. The big question that needs answering is 'how' a young athlete can work towards the highest levels of physical performance, commensurate with modern-day goalkeepers.

Working with any young athlete of 9-14 years of age, for example, is a crucial time to develop basic athletic competency. This will put them in a good position when more specific demands are placed upon them. Squatting, lunging, jumping/landing, running and basic bodyweight strength exercises are essential at this age.

All these basic movement patterns give a solid foundation to develop performance from. In addition, they set the athlete up in regard to *trainability* when the right time presents itself for strength training. Without reinforcing these fundamental areas, you may find yourself playing catch-up, which is always difficult with the demands of a high-level schedule.

Another pertinent area which must be included across all ages is flexibility and mobility.

Young athletes will be growing at different rates, and this growth can be massively detrimental to performance. We sometimes see a reduction in mobility and a reduction in flexibility during growth phases/growth spurts. At every contact, whether it is a technical or physical session, dynamic flexibility/mobility should be conducted pre-session, and developmental flexibility should be completed post-session.

Task

As a coach, if you're working with a group of goalkeepers of varying ages, have a go at mapping a long-term plan for them, with an individual focus for each player. Look at this holistically and not just from a physical perspective. This can give a good indication to the player what their long-term future might look like, and allows for plans to be created to bridge any performance gaps.

Motivated

It's not just applicable to football, or more specifically goalkeeping, but motivation in any sport has been found to be of fundamental importance in stimulating success in performance and training.

Goalkeepers need to be motivated; it's an essential ingredient for a successful performance between the sticks. Keepers must be motivated to take to the field on a cold, wet morning on a churned-up pitch, behind a dodgy defence, or when they are about to face the league leaders.

Motivation is a combination of the drive within us to achieve our aims and the outside factors which affect it. Motivation in sport can be defined, in a simple way, as the direction and intensity of individual effort, and it is key for determining *why* athletes do anything within sport.

Motivation has the following two forms: intrinsic motivation and extrinsic motivation. Intrinsic motivation is an inbuilt desire to become competent enough to master specific tasks. It is all about learning, developing, having fun, playing for pride, and being the best goalkeeper that you can possibly be. It is about the joy and satisfaction of participating and competing. It's about improving on your past goalkeeping performances. It's about *you* and not about the opposition.

Extrinsic motivation, on the other hand, is all about the glory, the plaudits, the medals, the trophies, and maybe even the fame and fortune. The motivation comes from other people. It's all about the winning; sometimes at all costs. It's about the result. It's about your opponents and not about you.

For a goalkeeper to improve the mental side of his game, it is important that she or he understands both intrinsic and extrinsic motivation. Intrinsic motivation is what is required for sustained long-term success; as a goalkeeper you need to love what you do. Extrinsic motivation also has its benefits, but usually just for the short term and as long as it is not overused.

Reliance on extrinsic motivation will not sustain goalkeeping success, as external rewards will not maintain motivation over the long haul. You need to supplement one with the other.

Intrinsic motivation must be the major factor for long-term sporting success. Learn to love goalkeeping. Unfortunately, in football, as in most sports, the tendency is to focus too much time on motivating athletes extrinsically – with trophies, medals, certificates, prize money, and so on. As a goalkeeper, do not put too much focus on these status symbols. And if you are a coach, play down these external rewards and do not use them as a carrot for your goalkeepers.

Instead, create a fun learning environment that encourages and praises improvements in personal goalkeeper performance and development – not just the results.

Being able to see *how*, *why*, and to *what* level goalkeepers are motivated is vital for coaches because it allows them to help their players reach their goals. For example, laying on extra challenging training or offering external rewards, as discussed.

A well-known professional goalkeeper once said to me… "I love football. I love playing. When I am not playing, I want to lie down and often think and remind myself what I have done, what I have sacrificed to get to that point in my career, and how much it makes my family proud when they come and watch me play."

Movement

Within my own coaching, I am a massive supporter of focusing on *how* and *when* a goalkeeper moves. My training practices reflect this in terms of design and the outcomes present. I like to give goalkeepers the opportunity to practise what they'd perform in a game, plus the opportunity to experiment with different kinds of patterns. I like making training scenario-based. An example would be to expose the goalkeeper to second-phase situations, so if they don't secure the ball, what do they have to do in order to protect the goal after the initial save?

Performance indicators would consist of: How do they get off the ground? What movements do they make – towards the goal or towards the ball? How and when do they travel around the goalmouth?

The term biomechanics can also transfer to this section. In simple terms, biomechanics can be defined as the study of the mechanics of human movement.

Within goalkeeping, there are various movement skills that the player needs to master. The most obvious are fundamental motor skills, such as jumping, kicking, throwing, and catching, which make up the majority of the goalkeeper's movements when faced with common situations in a match, such as shots on goal, distribution, and crosses.

The movements that goalkeepers make can be classified as 'non-linear' and 'irregular', which means a keeper must be able to control their body in every possible direction. In developing functional strength, the body will work in its natural freedom rather than a single plane of motion, which will aid the goalkeeper's movements through a more flexible state.

The ultimate aim is to get the goalkeeper moving from A to B as quickly as possible – along with developing how they coordinate and balance their body to make diving saves, jump through players, and change direction quickly. For example, moving across the goal area and re-positioning are frequent movements, and creating overload environments will get the goalkeeper used to moving quickly.

Moving across the goal can take many forms – some coaches use side steps, some use lateral running, and some advocate crossing over, but again it's up to the goalkeeper to use whatever method is comfortable and appropriate for them. Rhythm and timing are crucial in this respect.

The development of these specific movement skills and patterns needs to be supplemented by a bespoke physical training plan involving strength, stability, and speed exercises.

Nerve, Strength of

Being nervous or experiencing pressure is totally normal. Butterflies in the stomach, sweating, and general uptightness are commonplace at all levels of the game. Nerves stem from thought processes. It is, therefore, essential that your thought processes are positive; otherwise, the mind can run havoc.

Many believe 'strength of mind' is something you're born with. It isn't. Many will adopt a character that will see them succeed in 'pressure' situations, but this can be learned, worked on, and improved, like any other skill.

Combine positive images with powerful self-talk, eliminate all negativity, and see how great you can feel. The reality isn't always what your mind thinks it to be; you have the ability to create your own reality. Make it a good place to be. Watching videos and recounting past great performances can alleviate doubts for sure.

From my experience, the nerves I faced whilst playing were born from caring about the result and my performance – wanting to do well for my teammates, coaching staff, and myself. What could go wrong were the main headlines in my mind, not what could go right.

Another slant on 'nerves' is having the courage to fulfil a certain game plan. An example of this would be to play short into players under pressure and to receive under pressure – similar to how Manchester City under Pep Guardiola looks to play. This takes strength of nerve to carry out; the risk of failure with this task can be pretty high.

Another variation of this would be coping with different match situations. An example would be keeping a cool and steady head if your team is 1-0 up with five minutes to go, or if you're playing in a match that has more meaning on it, such as a cup final or the final match of the season where the league title is on the line.

Neuer, Manuel

A German goalkeeping legend, Manuel Neuer has followed in the footsteps of brilliant German keepers such as Oliver Khan and Jens Lehmann.

His proactive and – at times – risky approach to goalkeeping revolutionised the position in terms of managers wanting their keepers to defend the space *behind the defence,* and play as a sweeper keeper.

His ability to 'read the game' set him apart from other keepers while he was in his prime. Combine this with his incredible speed and agility, and his style of goalkeeping would be copied the world over by young players.

Neuer's ability to understand where to position himself, how he can benefit the team, and what to do in different situations would make him a massive asset for Bayern Munich and the German national team. Let's have a look at some of the factors he needs to consider to be the best *out of possession* goalkeeper in the modern game.

How to train like Neuer…

The basics of goalkeeping play, when out of possession, are made up of various parts, depending on the format, the level, and how a team approaches the game. In turn, out of possession competency gets greater with experience! This is because the player builds up a library of scenarios and pictures in their memory of how to deal with different types of attacks, patterns of play, cues to come up, cues to stay back, and how to communicate with teammates. From a novice player's perspective, it's essential that they are exposed to different trial and error experiences on how to perform when out of possession.

The main content will be around positioning (away from the ball) and not necessarily saving shots or dealing with crosses at this point. Psychological aspects such as concentration, focus, and attention play a massive role in this competence. Young players often need to develop these skills!

The next figure shows a simple picture where the opposition have the ball without any pressure on them; this opens up the possibility of playing in behind the goalkeeper's defensive line.

It's now common for goalkeepers to be responsible for protecting the marked space, dealing with balls that come over or through the backline. The higher you go up in football, the more complex this responsibility becomes, but from a simple 7v7 youth football perspective, the following is a good place to start when building a goalkeeper's understanding.

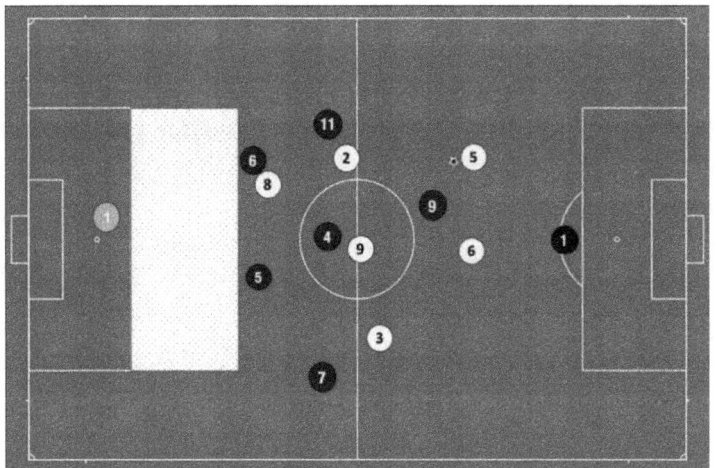

The next figure shows a situation where the goalkeeper is in an advanced position to protect the space behind their backline. The ultimate aim is to stop attacks and see/alleviate danger before it happens. With a goalkeeper fulfilling this role, the team can then be set up safe in the knowledge that this space is protected, and they may well be able to play more expansively.

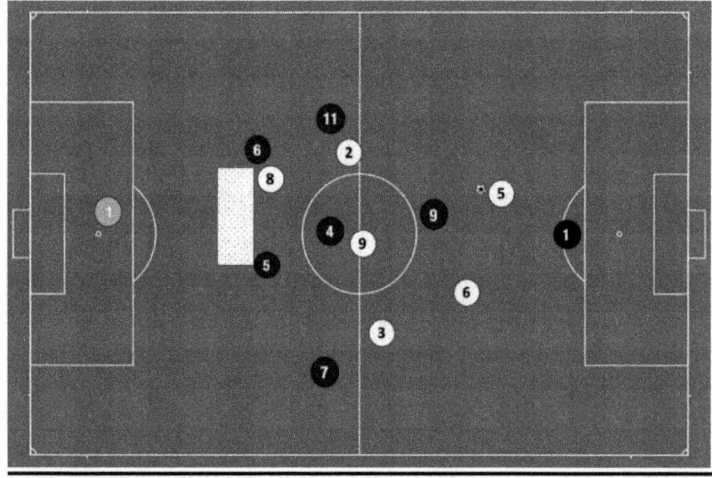

Figure 3 shows the importance of playing 'ball-side' and 'defending the gaps' between players. Here the goalkeeper is looking to be on the same side of the ball, so they can be in a proactive, front-foot position in order to protect any passes into the shaded area – which is a dangerous place for the opposition to have the ball.

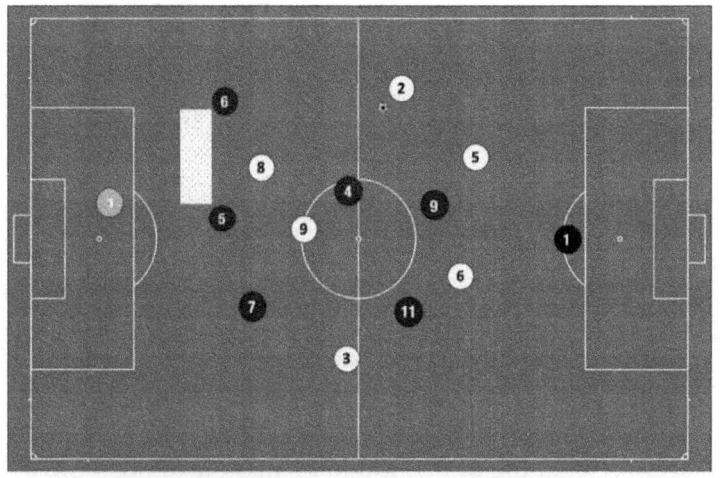

When an opposition sees a front-foot and aware goalkeeper, they will be less inclined to play defence-splitting passes and typically look for a different or more patient opening.

Moving on, the emphasis will now be more on the 11v11 format, although the above principles transfer directly to every format.

In the following figure, a few things can be noted.

- See where the 9 is. The opposition will usually look to get their offensive players into the game by getting the ball into players to link – trying to play around the sides for final third entries or playing in behind to exploit any space. From a goalkeeping perspective, it's beneficial to see how a team is attacking and where their main threats are. In this case, the point of seeing where the 9 is, is to anticipate where the opposition might play and to look to nullify that through a positive starting position. In the figure, the goalkeeper is patrolling the area into which the ball might be played

(whether into the 9 or over the 9 to run onto). If the ball position changes, the goalkeeper's positioning will evolve in order to see and counter the new problem.
- Opposition target players/areas. This relates closely to the above, but the difference is being able to adapt to identified opposition players and their main threats. Of course, at the top end of the game, teams will know how sides attack and/or approach the game, but at youth or amateur level, this level of intel isn't necessarily available.

An example of this might be that the opposition looks to target playing in-between the centre-backs and full-backs. If this is the case, the goalkeeper must look to defend this space from through balls and final third entries to nullify and cut out danger.
- Transition. With the pace of the game becoming quicker and more dynamic, the goalkeeper must be tuned into the speed of the play in front of them. The notion of transition – in this case, attack turning into defence – allows the goalkeeper to embrace the responsibility of being wise to counterattacks and fast-breaking attacks. The vital way in which the goalkeeper can be ultra-effective is to hold their position up the pitch in order to protect the space in front of them, rather than retreating to protect the goal. The priority, at this point, is not to protect the goal but to look to stop threats coming towards them.
- Concentration | Awareness | Proactivity – three buzz words that look to sum up a goalkeeper's out of position mindset. Keepers need to be active and alive when out of possession. They should always be thinking about "What if?".

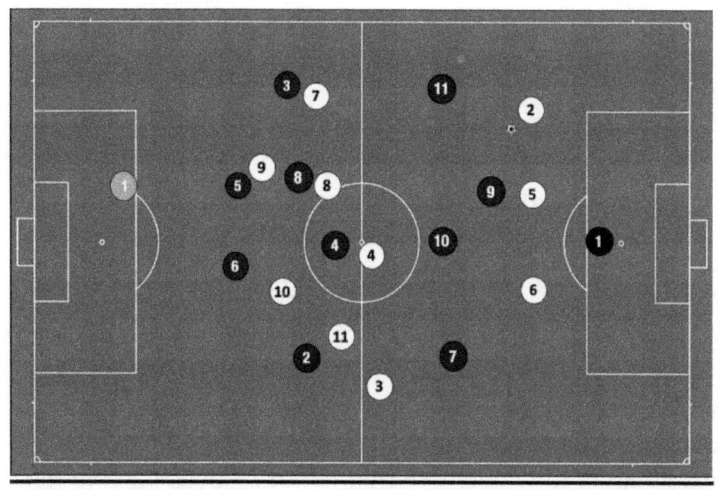

The below figure relates to the above words. The keeper must show concentration when the opposition attack, an awareness of any changes in opposition positioning, and be proactive to sense and cut out any danger.

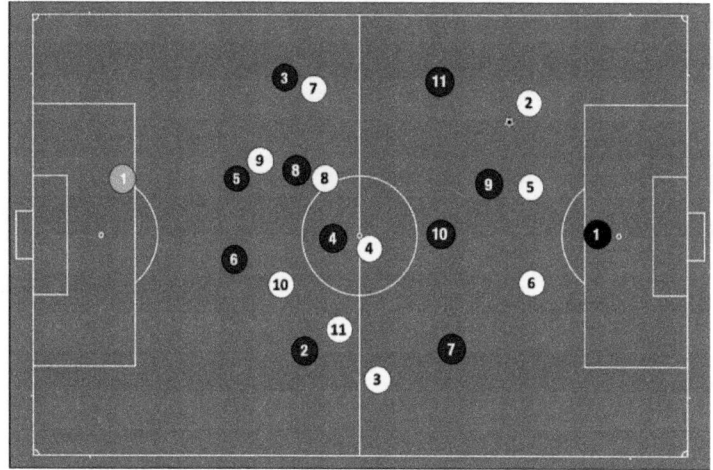

The questions to ask yourself when your team is out of possession revolve around the following:

- What is my job at this moment in time?
- Do I need to protect the space in front of me?
- Do I need to give information to my team?
- Am I taking up a position to stop the opposition playing a certain type of pass?
- Am I preparing to protect the goal?

There is a multitude of questions that can run through a goalkeeper's mind – but the most important thing for a keeper to remember is to do *YOUR* job and not be distracted by too many external factors. Focus on *yourself* and what *you* can control in any given situation.

With pressure off the ball, there can be an immediate threat in behind the defence or, if further forward, on their goal. This may make the goalkeeper wary of advancing too high or being too gung-ho. With pressure on the ball, the team are able to creep up the pitch or slide across the pitch to nullify the opposition. The figure below shows a scenario where there is no great amount of pressure on the ball, and there is a threat of running behind (in the form of the number 10).

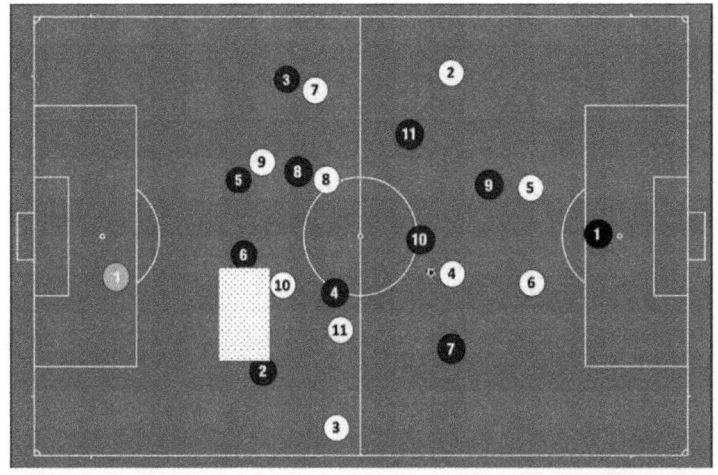

The goalkeeper must now think, can the opposition shoot? Most probably not. So, will the ball go towards the willing runner? Yes, and the keeper needs to be in a position to deal with the ball into the shaded zone. If they can't affect the ball directly, they'll need to be able to drop quickly towards the goal to then cope with what comes next. This could take the form of having to make a 1v1 block when advancing, setting deep to save a shot, or – if a defender secures the ball – being able to retain the ball and build an attack.

Never Beaten

A huge bugbear of mine when coaching is when goalkeepers don't make an attempt to try and save the ball, or give up on the ball.

This portrays negative body language in terms of not caring nor taking pride in protecting their goal. Something that needs to be instilled – in every goalkeeper – is a mentality of *never being beaten* and *going for everything*.

This stems from a desire to protect the goal at all costs; it's a mentality that gets inspired and cemented during training sessions.

In my experience, from working with numerous outfield coaches, four things create a really positive impression: a goalkeeper showing passion in defending their goal, a goalkeeper who puts their body on the line, a goalkeeper who gets annoyed at conceding, and a goalkeeper who strives to work for the team. By definition, the opposite to the above qualities suggests laziness.

Number 2

Being able to deal with competition is part and parcel of the position; only one person can play at any one time and the prospect of sitting on the bench is not something to be relished.

A big part of development is being able to deal with adversity, setbacks, and tough situations. Not playing, playing half a match, or being replaced by another player are common scenarios that many goalkeepers face and have to be able to deal with. From a coaching perspective, it's important you support the goalkeeper. Be honest and explain situations – communication breakdowns or misunderstandings are the common denominators when problems arise. I've learned lessons from this!

Drip-feeding this in the right way, from a young age, will produce goalkeepers that are aware of the nature of the position and who are able to deal with setbacks as they get older. For example, a young goalkeeper going into a first-team environment where they may not play will need to sit on the bench and bide their time. This is natural in the development pathway; the key is to take all experiences on board and learn from them. Hard work, patience, and trusting the process are required.

Tournament football is another aspect of the number 2 goalkeeper. Usually, during a tournament competition at most levels, there will be a 'visible' number 1, with the others providing backup. This role has a separate skillset in itself. One where they provide support, motivation, and encouragement to the starting player. Indeed, goalkeepers that are selected to go away to tournaments are, at times, selected to be part of the squad, based upon qualities that lend themselves to the skillset mentioned. This is done to harmonise the goalkeeping unit and make sure that each goalkeeper knows their role within the group.

Optimal Performance

Optimal performance is all about what needs to be in place for a goalkeeper to perform at their best; to enter the pitch feeling like a million dollars.

It can be hard to separate life and football. Going out to play and forgetting about daily life and focusing solely on a match comes a lot easier to some than others. Focusing on what the player can control is, of course, vital.

Worrying about too many external factors – that are not controllable – clouds judgement and confuses the mind. The goalkeeper needs to have total clarity on what they have been asked to do in possession of the ball. How have I been asked to exploit the opposition? How are we playing from goal kicks? In an ideal world, these would have been worked on in the days leading up to the match. With this clarity comes the ability to play freely and without inhibitions.

The player needs to know that the coaches have their back. If the player sticks to the game plan, then no matter what mistakes happen, things will be okay. This leads to optimal performance.

Task

Provide your goalkeepers with a match script. How do you want them to play the ball from the back? What areas do you want to exploit to impact the opposition? What spaces do they need to protect that the defence can't cover? The answers to these questions provide role clarity.

Own The Penalty Area

My yard; the penalty area is my yard. The 18-yard box should give the goalkeeper a sense of ownership that 'this is their domain'. They take control of what happens there, and they won't let the opposition occupy and take advantage of this part of the pitch.

Like a general leading their troops into battle, they must command and take responsibility for situations – snuffing out opportunities to attack their goal. Many of the qualities and characteristics written about in this book contribute towards achieving this ownership – they include being vocal, understanding their role, showing speed and strength, nerve strength, and intelligence.

Goalkeepers must step up to the plate and become leaders. Ownership is 9/10 of the law; make sure the goalkeeper doesn't forget that.

Playing

The best way to get better as a goalkeeper… is to play. No amount of on-pitch or off-the-pitch work can substitute for what is learnt on gameday.

Playing provides the chance to implement what you've been training hard to learn and achieve; it is the pinnacle of the week and what everything is built around. For a coach, game day is when their plans come to fruition.

Not playing games can take different forms. But no one ever got better sitting on a bench. The modern seats in the dugouts might be heated and comfy, but this comfort is misplaced. Getting game time might involve moving clubs, going out on loan, or playing in the reserve/B team.

In the end, each player needs to take ownership of not playing. Am I doing all I can to play? Can I train better? Can I work on x and y to get in the team? All of these are questions that a player can ask themselves; they also need to get honest feedback from the decision-makers. Don't get splinters sitting on the bench!

Power

Power, in short, is the combination of speed and strength. This is a pre-requisite of being able to cover the goal and takes a long time to develop, especially through the formative years before turning 18. This looks different for male and female goalkeepers, as well, because of their physical/genetic makeup.

Muscle power is a function of the interaction between force of contraction and the speed of contraction, and is associated with the explosiveness of the muscle. The relationship between force and speed of contraction and the subsequent point at which peak power occurs varies between athletes, with peak power occurring at 50–70% of the maximum weight that can be lifted for one repetition.

A fundamental way of increasing muscle power is to increase maximal strength, particularly in untrained athletes. However, as stated above, this may not be the best method of training goalkeepers.

For most athletes, increasing muscular power is a primary goal. Despite a relationship between power and strength training, power is a separate component, and any training programme must be adjusted when working on power. Strength training forms the basis of muscle power and also forms the basis of most sporting abilities to a large extent.

Power has been identified as a vital component in jumping, based on the fact that a superior ability to execute the movement *explosively* typically results in a more desirable performance.

Speaking to a Norwegian Athletics coach once, I was told that the highest score on the vertical jump test came from a sprinter!

Punching

Punching is a skill that's somewhat come back into fashion in recent years. Back in the day, when keepers didn't wear gloves, and there was a high level of physical contact, keepers would regularly punch or divert the ball away, so they didn't get hit or taken down by an onrushing opponent.

Then there was a period when keepers were expected to catch everything, regardless of the situation. Two attackers near you, catch it! Knocked off balance and falling over, catch it! If you could get two hands to the ball, you could catch it.

Some key details on punching depend largely on the situation the keeper finds themselves in, rather than a pre-determined decision that they're definitely going to punch the ball before a cross is delivered, for example.

Punching – One-Handed Punch

What

The one-handed punch is an action designed to deal (predominantly) with an aerial ball. It's a physical action that requires a high amount of coordination and controlled aggressive intent. Without this intent, a punch turns into more of a poke. Being able to effectively clear danger with a punch will help the defence build trust towards the goalkeeper and know that the team has a presence that can help alleviate pressure.

When

This is used when the goalkeeper has decided that they can't cleanly claim the ball. The idea is to affect the ball to release the danger and clear the ball to safety – much like a centre-half heading the ball away.

The action can be used when coming in front of players, travelling away from players, or within a physical duel – as shown in the images.

One should try to avoid a one-handed punch when coming for crosses within the width of the goal. This is due to the difficult nature of the technique and *where* the action is taking place. A more secure alternative would be better, such as the two-handed punch. It offers a more controlled and stable action.

How

Imagine a boxer punching an opponent with a big right hand; this is the exact same motion. Rather than extending the arms at head or body level, however, a goalkeeper should punch so that the hand finishes above their head; they're effectively punching upwards.

The detail is to punch the back of the ball with a clenched fist, and look to make clean contact.

This contact can take the ball either away from the direction it has come from, or back towards it – it depends largely on the pace and flight of the ball. If the ball is softly flighted, then there isn't the requisite pace to help the ball away from goal. This example would require more of a jumping action through the ball – as shown in the first image.

The second image shows more of a physical duel where the goalkeeper has been caught under the flight of the ball, and needs to reach to use their right hand (furthest away) to help the ball away from the goal.

Regardless of how the punch is executed, the assessment of the ball and the timing of the action is absolutely vital.

Tactically, once the punch has been performed – no matter where or how this is done – the goalkeeper must retreat back to the goal line. This is because there will likely be a second phase to deal with. This could be another attack to face, an immediate shot, a set play to organise the team for, or their team secures possession of the ball.

Punching - Two-Handed Punch

What

The two-handed punch is an action that is used to clear the ball far away from where the goalkeeper deals with it.

The party line from a lot of managers is that if the goalkeeper can get two hands to the ball, they should be able to catch it! Now on the surface, this seems a reasonable shout. But when you investigate what goes into this type of action, it's clear that each event needs to be taken on its own merits. By this, I mean that even if the goalkeeper manages to get two hands to the ball, they may not be able to secure the ball, due to being off-balance because of late physical contact or having mishandled the ball.

When

This is best used when the goalkeeper is either under pressure or is moving towards the ball. The first image, below, depicts the goalkeeper moving fast and late through the ball with both fists. Notice how the attacking player is behind the keeper, which means the keeper can't exactly see where they are. As such, the two-handed punch would be an appropriate option in this situation.

Also, if the goalkeeper has decided that they're going to claim the ball, both their hands will naturally be ready to do a two-handed punch. If there is a change in the situation (for example, the ball catches the wind, or a player moves late towards them), they can adjust their decision and use both their hands to execute the punch, rather than the claim.

How

Much like the one-handed punch, the action relies on a high amount of coordination and controlled aggressive intent.

The goalkeeper needs to time their jump *into* the ball – and then follow through – in order to get the most power and momentum through the ball to create the distance on the ball. A double-legged jump allows for this thrust through the ball – giving the goalkeeper more of a balanced, stable base to work from.

Tactically, as with the one-handed punch, once the punch has been performed, no matter where or how this is done, the goalkeeper must retreat back to the goal line, as there will likely be a second phase to deal with.

Training practice

Description

1. The ball is delivered towards the goalkeeper and the two mannequins as a flat serve – this can be with feet or hands.
2. The goalkeeper looks to punch the ball into the two mini goals – which are in this position to show a

safe place for the ball to go to avoid a secondary attack.

Progressions

1. The wide player changes their position and the flight they put on the ball. Crosses with less pace on will be tougher to generate the necessary pace to reach the mini goals.
2. Add contact on the goalkeeper.

Main coaching points

- Decide on one or two-handed punches by assessing the situation.
- Speed and intent to meet the ball.
- Focus on the outcome of the punch (where the ball goes).

Quarterback

Fans of the NFL will be familiar with the role the quarterback plays in the sport. Also, readers of my previous books will be familiar with the term 'Terzino', which is Italian for quarterback – a name given to the goalkeeper's role in possession of the football.

The quarterback sees the whole game, just like the goalkeeper. They have the ability to pick passes, carry out strategic plays, and take a lead in team dynamics. The evolution of the role, as discussed earlier, empowers the goalkeeper to perform the quarterback role. Through intelligence, understanding the tactical implications of their position within the team, and being smart in their approach – just like the quarterback in the NFL – they'll become a vital cog in any side.

Task

Watch an NFL game or any other American Football format, or even clips on the internet, and observe the quarterback. Ask yourself these questions to begin with: What kind of decisions are they making? What information are they taking in? What kind of passes are they looking for? This could also be a task set by a coach for a player. Or indeed a discussion between the both of them.

Questions

For a goalkeeper, *asking questions* is crucial. Due to the random and varied nature of the position, the need to be curious, try out new techniques, and generally be ready to extract information from other players and coaches should be high on the agenda.

In my coaching environments, I always try to bring in a scholar (a 16–18-year-old) or a young professional to assist in the coaching of the younger players. I encourage the young players to pick the older player's brains to try and get an insight into the possible situations they will encounter.

Ultimately, the younger players are striving to be where the older players are. First-hand descriptions of making their way in the youth game can quell worries and provide advice. Questions might revolve around, 'How do you prepare for games when you get older?', 'What should I eat before training sessions?', 'How can I get signed for a scholarship?' and 'How can I improve my kicking before I get to under 16s?'. These are all questions I've heard asked before.

As a player, the objective is to become an independent learner and decision-maker. Eking out knowledge from coaches is a great approach; asking questions and being curious will speed up the process of becoming a capable goalkeeper.

Realistic Practices

Looking at the way goalkeepers are coached, I believe there is more we could add to practices that better prepare them for the main event… the match. This preparation includes training the movements that keepers are likely to make in a match (rather than traditionally taught footwork patterns and prescribed handling drills).

The position encompasses so many dynamic and irregular body positions (or technical adaptability and improvisation) that the modern-day goalkeeper must be trained in a more diverse environment where they can be creative and work out the best way to deal with any given match situation. Remember – every shot or event is different in some shape or form.

When to work on different goalkeeping topics and *how* far in advance to plan development programmes are common discussions. Should coaches plan every week, every four weeks, every six weeks, every three months, or even plan the whole season? Every coach will have a different cycle of working, but what I would say is *keep it flexible* and focus clearly on what each goalkeeper at your disposal needs in order to develop fully as a player and as a young person.

A lot of training environments I've seen in the past (and even been a part of playing-wise) are too comfortable for the goalkeeper and don't leave them striving for improvements. This leaves very limited or non-existent decision-making opportunities.

For young goalkeepers and novices, the environment could be a bit more structured at first, but as skill and proficiency levels increase, challenge individuals and take them out of their comfort zones. In training, they should make mistakes; if you're learning a new skill or movement, this is expected. Finding the balance between quantity and quality of practice is also crucial.

Coaches can get caught up in a methodical, prescriptive manner: "The ball goes there – make this save; the ball goes there – make that save." In reality, goalkeeping is far more complex, and training should incorporate a large proportion of reactive and anticipation-oriented exercises.

In turn, don't be scared by spending time during each session on the basics (to get a goalkeeper's eye in, during the warm-up).

Some of the time, I see a jovial atmosphere at training where the coach has laid on 'easy to coach' drills; where they know which technical points to teach and when. I ask you to open your eyes and observe and tailor your training programmes to what happens in a match. Make sessions realistic, relevant, and appropriate!

Practice

Description

The above practice is based around three goalkeepers, and the passage of the practice is based on a super strength attribute.

- Service 1 is a touch past a mannequin with a strike on goal from 12-14 yards.
- Service 2 is a high-diving save.
- Service 3 is a low-diving save.

Progressions

Adjustments can be made by making the service more random or changing serving positions/types.

Main coaching points

Within a super strength session, the main interventions should be around reminders and affirmations of key technical and physical detail – this will allow the goalkeepers to be free of mental overload; they can express themselves in something they are excellent at.

Reflexes

A goalkeeper with the ability to make incredible saves might be seen as having amazing reflexes. The qualities here can be seen as a blend of flexibility, power, balance, agility, and explosive coordination.

Reflex training consists of not only physical training but also how fast the mind can process what the body needs to do, responding accordingly.

A practical example of this would be a keeper seeing a ball crossed into the area, assessing whether they can directly affect the ball (position + flight of the ball, and player positioning), deciding they cannot, and then finding the optimum position to defend the goal, observing that a shot on goal is going to take place and then taking in all the visual information present to then decide how they can save the ball.

The reason why reflex saves look so 'instinctive' is because they've been practised hundreds of times on the training pitch – giving the goalkeeper a memory bank of saves to fall back on and use when needed.

Schmeichel, Peter & Kasper

They are, no doubt, the most famous father-and-son goalkeeping duo that the football world has ever seen.

Following in a famous footballing father's footsteps can't be easy, but Kasper Schmeichel has made a stellar career for himself, winning the Premier League with Leicester City and winning many international caps for Denmark.

His father, Peter Schmeichel, changed the perception of goalkeeping from the early 90s with his incredible athleticism (even though he was 6ft 4in) and his ability to make '*Unorthodox Saves*'.

Kasper, despite being different in stature, has carried on his father's legacy in bringing a unique and impulsive style to goalkeeping.

How to train like a Schmeichel

What

The 'Star Save', as discussed, was made famous by the great Dane, Peter Schmeichel – and carried on by his son Kasper, the Premier League-winning goalkeeper for Leicester City and current Danish number 1. A save that is explosive in nature and which requires bravery to the nth degree.

When

The star spread is what you might call a last resort! Or to use an American Football term, a Hail Mary! It might be used during the following situations:

- When the goalkeeper is scrambling across the goal and throws themselves towards the opposing player.
- When there is a bouncing ball within the goalmouth, and both players (goalkeeper and opposition) are in close vicinity to the ball.
- From a crossed ball, an opposing player has a clear, unopposed finish, and the goalkeeper has a final option to try to just *get something* on the ball to affect the finish.

- When the ball is central, in relation to the goal, and the goalkeeper is looking to make themselves as imposing as possible to try to either affect the ball or put off the opposing player.

How

The above image shows the keeper's star shape, and the action just after the ball has struck the goalkeeper's leg. The goalkeeper is central in the goal, as he had made the star block to try to get any touch on the ball. From this central position, the opposing player is clear to score (to either side of the keeper) and should do so nine times out of ten! The keeper is looking to make their body as imposing and large as possible to make the save.

The next image is a slightly different situation, where the ball is closer to the ground. (It could be argued that this should invoke a different type of block to the star one.) But, with the position of the opposing player – six yards out and in the centre of the goal – the odds are very much in their favour. So, a star spread is the best available option here due to the fact the keeper can make their upper body as big a barrier as possible, and they can try to cover as much of the goal as they can.

Training practices

Description

1. Both of the above practices have the same outcomes, in the fact that the ball is played into the attacker from different ball positions each time.

2. The ball is played into the attacker or into the space around them. They then attack the goal with the goalkeeper having to deny them in an appropriate manner. The emphasis will be on how quickly the attacker can finish – due to the fact that, in a games-based practice, there will be recovering defenders looking to win the ball from them.

3. In the need for realism, give the attacker the objective of finishing as quickly as possible and at 'match pace'. Also, you could give the attacker a touch or time limit as a constraint.

Progressions

1. Play second phases after the goalkeeper has saved the ball.

2. Add in a defender to increase complexity and to give the goalkeeper the decision of attacking the ball or protecting the goal.

Main coaching points

- Can the goalkeeper delay the attacker for a necessary amount of time in order for teammates to recover (without defenders, this scenario can be created through time constraints)?

- In terms of goalkeeping actions, use the above information to help guide the observation and intervention process towards the goalkeeper. Are they engaging the ball at the right time and using the most effective action given the situation?

- The key is to allow the goalkeeper to experiment with different techniques, actions, and movements – this way, they can find their own way to make saves and bring a sense of individuality to dealing with a 1v1 situation. This would relate to all the above saving actions within 1v1s.

Securing The Ball

Securing the ball as a goalkeeper makes life much easier; a) they have the ball to start an attack, b) the pressure is off the defence, and c) they haven't conceded.

There are many times when keepers aren't able to catch or secure the ball. Contributing factors include the distance of the strike on goal, the speed of the ball, if the ball has curve/spin on it, if the ball is deflected and changes direction quickly, and weather/pitch conditions like dew and rain.

In an ideal world, the keeper would catch the ball all the time, every time! And many managers and coaches would love this, of course. The common-sense approach would be to take every situation on its merits rather than a blanket approach. What all these saves have in common is that the keeper must be able to get the ball away from immediate danger (such as an easy tap-in or a second-phase opposition play). Using the penalty area as a reference point is useful, and employing the term 'clear the box', provides the goalkeeper with a clear, unequivocal ethos.

Training the ability to secure the ball, like any action, is a skill in itself. Coaches' practices should build this skill into the objectives and provide guidance on how to secure the ball effectively. It has to be the *first thought* when presented with the ball, and the goalkeeper can then work backwards from this starting point and assess if they need to deflect or push the ball away.

Set Plays

A set play is a restart in football. These include corner kicks, free kicks, throw-ins, and penalties… and (for some) goal kicks, which is a nuance to many coaches. More on this to come.

Set plays are usually pre-planned. Practised in the days leading up to a game and specifically designed around the team's strengths and preferences, and the opposition's dangers, they are likened to a 'playbook' as seen in American Football. Premier League clubs at first team level, are now employing specialist set play coaches, such is the importance placed upon them. After all, these situations are an unopposed possession!

From a goalkeeper's perspective, defending set plays is something they take a leading role in. This revolves around organising, giving information, and implementing a desired setup. Keepers also need to spot danger and the main threats from the opposition. Other situations include deciding how many players are in a wall, lining up the wall, and where the defensive line should start. Set plays conclude with the standard situations that a goalkeeper will face, such as crosses, reaction saves, and long-range shots on goal.

The emphasis placed on the goalkeeper to affect the ball varies from team to team, depending on who's between the sticks. If a goalkeeper is aerially dominant, then the team would be set up to allow the goalkeeper to come for the ball. This would include setting up teammates to block players to give the keeper a clearer path to the ball, and having players on the post to cover the goal if the keeper leaves the line.

The flip side is for goalkeepers who are reluctant to become involved in aerial contests. Here, the team would need to be set up to counterbalance the keeper's reticence by having players who are good in the air positioned around the goal to attack the ball. The ins and outs of set plays depend on the team – with age, gender, and format influencing the different approaches.

From an attacking viewpoint, many teams place their goalkeeper well outside their penalty area in order to defend the space from any counterattacks. Looking at the modern game, teams can go from defending their own penalty area to having a shot on goal in a matter of seconds, such is the pace and directness of current forwards.

Revisiting the goal kick example (from the first paragraph), a goal kick should be considered a set play, in my opinion. It's a restart, it can be pre-planned and practised, and it's unopposed – all the characteristics of other set plays.

In contemporary play, teams use goal kicks to build attacks through pre-planned tactics, which includes specific positioning and frequent practice in training. The goalkeeper is the first line of the attacking system!

Strength + Speed

Strength

Strength in the lower limbs is of obvious importance in football: the quadriceps and hamstring groups must generate high forces for jumping, kicking, tackling, turning, and changing pace.

The ability to sustain forceful contractions is also important in maintaining balance and control, especially when being challenged for possession. Isometric strength is a significant contributory factor in maintaining a player's balance on a slippery pitch and for ball control.

Combined with this, the goalkeeper must carry and control their body through non-linear motions, as discussed in the biomechanics section, so strength training must not be one dimensional and should be performed by putting the body through many different directions.

For a goalkeeper, almost all the body's muscle groups are important for executing positional skills. The vertical jump and short sprints are actions that require leg (gluteals, quadriceps, hamstrings) and core strength (abdominals and trunk muscles) training.

The term 'functional strength' (training the body for movements it performs in its sport, rather than simply isolating target muscle groups) highlights the fact that typical weight training exercises (for example, how many bench presses you can do) do not replicate sports-specific movements. The use of core stability methods such as medicine balls and dumbbells are very prominent. One research article found a 58% increase in strength over fixed-form programmes of weight training machines when using core stability techniques. They also found that these exercises can help work on power, flexibility, and balance. This type of training is recommended for explosive sports that require speed of movement.

Research suggests that the most important strength factor in goalkeeping is not that of the *maximal* kind, but functional type, from different starting positions. Using free weights would, therefore, increase the range of motion and promote muscle balance.

Moreover, elastic strength, being the ability to overcome resistance with a fast contraction, will help the goalkeeper in moving their hands and feet fast to react to the ball.

In any case, the key point is to use 'functional strength' during goalkeeping actions and to "make maximal use of the strength available."

Having good and effective core strength for a goalkeeper is vital. When these muscles contract, they stabilize areas of the body, such as the pelvis, spine, and shoulder girdle to create a solid support base.

When this occurs, a goalkeeper becomes able to generate powerful movements in his or her extremities. Basically, the core muscles stabilize and assist powerful movements because they all initiate from the centre of the body. Muscles here would include the abdominals, obliques, hip flexors, hip adductors, and gluteals. And, of course, training the core muscles will assist with injury prevention and aid with postural imbalances.

Speed

Physical speed and reaction time have been paired together because of the nature of quickness. 'Speed of body, speed of mind'. Reaction time would normally be considered a psychological attribute, but with its obvious physical implications in goalkeeping performance – it goes hand in hand with physical speed.

Speed can, in simple terms, be described as how quickly something gets from A to B. In goalkeeping terms, it relates to the time taken to come out for through balls, the time to re-position, the time to support the play, and the time to save the ball, of course. Lateral speed across the goal area and vertical speed towards the ball are commonly used measures (along with backwards speed to reposition) of performance.

If a goalkeeper is physically quick in all directions, it will give them a significant advantage. The key – when speed training any goalkeeper – is to improve acceleration (the first five yards). The goalkeeper will never really reach maximal speed because this occurs somewhere between 30-50 yards; a distance which they rarely, if ever, reach.

Keeping body movements short and concise will retain balance as well as enable the keeper to be in a position to 'set' at any point. If movements are too big, it will take longer to regain a set position and time to readjust if the ball changes direction. Physiology-wise, the key muscles used here would be the upper and lower leg muscles, along with the core and gluteals.

A simple and appropriate definition of reaction time would be the time that elapses between a stimulus and the response to it. I think it goes without saying that decreasing your goalkeeper's reaction time is of real benefit. Training should focus on decision-making scenarios (game-based theory) and the use of short, sharp goalmouth practice.

Practice

Description

1. A more prescribed practice due to its basic nature.
2. The goalkeeper will receive serves at each diving height, from different angles, in order to build familiarity with the required actions/movements.

Progressions

1. The serve can be throws, volleys, or ground strikes.
2. Random practice will help hone and develop a keeper's decision-making for what height to dive at.
3. Change the distances and angles so the goalkeeper can get used to how the body's responses need to change when the ball is hit from different locations – in terms of dive angle.

Main coaching points

- Observe the height of the dive. Is it appropriate for the ball, and does the centre of mass/head get as close to the ball as possible?
- Is the player taking the ball in front of the body?
- Is the keeper going with one or two hands to make contact with the ball?

- If the keeper takes hold of the ball, are they holding on to it when they hit the ground upon landing? The landing can cause the ball to spill out of their hands due to the force/impact on the floor.

Transitions

Transitions happen in many invasion games, and they sway momentum in matches.

A transition in football can be defined as "the process of recognising and responding – in the first few seconds – after losing or regaining possession of the football." In recent years, teams at the highest level of football have recognised this phase as a way of gaining a competitive advantage over their opponents.

Transitions can be separated into: 1. attack to defence, and 2. defence to attack, and the goalkeeper's role in this facet of the game has become increasingly important as tactics have evolved.

When defending against a transition, the goalkeeper must be aware, firstly, *where* the transition has taken place. The following will give some examples.

- **In their defensive third:** be prepared to defend the goal right away, from a fast attack or a long-range shot. Information given here needs to be sharp and concise due to the emergency nature of the situation. The keeper's team would be positioned to retain the ball or build an attack, so the distances

between players would normally be larger than if they were compactly defending. A transition in the defensive third makes the defence unit easier to penetrate, given the larger spaces created.
- **In their midfield third:** more often, if a change of possession occurs in this area of the field, the opposition would look to either be patient and stay on the ball or look to slide passes forward earlier for forward runners. In the first instance, the goalkeeper must position themselves on the front foot in order to affect any of these slide passes, which would take the form of through balls. If the opposition is patient, then instructing players to get compact and back into shape is the priority. Having a proactive mindset and body position will give the keeper a head start.
- **In their attacking third:** there is no immediate danger of an attack here, unless you're playing Man City or PSG, of course. Best of luck defending the space against Kylian Mbappe. So, the priority is to make sure the backline is secure by ensuring defenders are in the right position to protect from a fast attack. The keeper needs to again be proactive with their positioning, looking to defend the gaps between their defence and the space behind them.

The best exponents of these three transitions – in the male game right now – are Manuel Neuer and Hugo Lloris.

A lot of the strategies depend, of course, on how the keeper's team is playing in terms of their general strategy or the match situation. If their 1-0 up in the last minute, then the likelihood of their team pressing high is quite low.

From an attacking point of view, the transition images that stick in my mind are a Peter Schmeichel long throw to Ryan Giggs in the mid to late 90s, or a Pepe Reina side volley to Luis Garcia or Fernando Torres. The idea of exploiting the opposition while they are out of shape is not a new phenomenon. This happens when the goalkeeper gets possession of the ball from a set play or an open play attack, too. Looking for 1v1s or 2v2s further up the pitch is a good visual prompt for the keeper.

Understanding The Position

Now, from my viewpoint – given what I've done and what I know – in order to understand the goalkeeping position fully, you really need to have played the position. This does not mean a handful of games or 100 caps for your country, but a time when you've dedicated a period of time to playing and training in the position.

You need to empathise with the pitfalls, the joys, the demands, the idiosyncrasies, and the responsibilities to fully understand what goes through keepers' minds.

But what about coaching the position? *Holistically*, in my opinion, it is best to have played the position.

Teaching basic techniques, of course, need not require playing time between the sticks, but how could someone give advice on how to recover after conceding a soft goal, or how to physically prepare for a game, if that someone hasn't been in that position before?

There are various goalkeeping topics you can learn about, through coaching courses, podcasts, and being around goalkeepers, but – without being in certain situations – it's extremely challenging to relate.

The same can be said for my own understanding. I've never played in front of 30,000 fans, so can I fully assist in helping a goalkeeper prepare for this kind of arena? I can give them strategies and ways to thrive, but can I really *feel* what they will/can feel? I'm not so sure.

Task

A great way to build game understanding is to watch football. This sounds simple, of course, but by watching different goalkeepers play, you can see what roles, responsibilities, and tasks they carry out.

It also provides the opportunity to see how they read the play and position themselves, and build awareness of what kinds of situations a goalkeeper might face.

Match analysis tasks and tactical discussions are powerful between the player and coach, so, where possible and feasible, employ them in the game understanding process.

Unique

Now, this meaning of unique doesn't indicate the uniqueness of the position (I think this has been well documented throughout the previous sections). This is more to do with how each goalkeeper *must* construct their own style of goalkeeping. Many a time, players are compared to other players – either of the current era or a previous time. It's cliché to say 'Player X is the new Player Z', for example. Similar traits can be seen in others for sure, but each goalkeeper needs to find their own way of how to keep goal, and every action that comes with it.

From a coaching perspective, this is crucial, and the player needs to be the centre of the process. In a nutshell, the coach must *facilitate* the process for the player to find their own identity as a footballer.

So many times, you will hear a young player say, "I want to play like Pickford, Ederson, Neuer, Donnarumma, etc." (which is great, don't get me wrong), but if you unpick what this really *means*, then you can delve into what makes up an individual goalkeeper, in terms of their goalkeeping characteristics and what makes them special.

Players form their own identities by watching role models, responding to their training environments, and heeding advice from others; in doing so, they form their own unique styles and approaches.

Vision

Vision and awareness are the difference makers at the elite level of the game. They are the most important yet often underdeveloped skills that a player can possess.

In football, when we talk about vision, we are referring to more than just 20/20 vision. We are referring to the foundations that the whole visual system is built upon – how good the quality of the information coming in is.

Have you ever considered that maybe the goalkeeper you are working with (the one that struggles so badly with crosses) maybe does not have a technical problem?

Visual Skills Training is largely based on training the muscles around the eyes to improve speed, endurance, and efficiency of movement. This is mostly done with computer-based training software or technology-based training equipment. The efficacy of such programs is still up for debate, with evidence both for and against; those who are sceptical say that athletes don't necessarily need better than average 'everyday' visual skills. But our players don't perform in the 'everyday' environment; they perform in a fast-paced, dynamic arena where key information is constantly changing.

The goalkeeper relies on being able to see and spot danger. They need to anticipate, react, and respond to a myriad of different situations. By building realistic practices into a session that involves the right ball and player movements, the keeper will quickly train how they can assess a situation – both in terms of what the situation is and what the ball is actually doing.

Vocal

A much-underestimated quality in goalkeeping is the ability to command, instruct, and organise those around them. This quality links to many of the sub-sections above, due to the fact that whatever role the goalkeeper is fulfilling, they are usually found communicating in some shape or form.

Being vocal doesn't mean just screaming and shouting in a non-coherent manner – but being calm, concise, and supplying useful information to those around them.

Being vocal is a skill that can be trained, but it also comes with the experience of different situations. Don't expect young keepers to suddenly enter the pitch and be an all-singing, all-dancing orchestrator of the team. There will be more extrovert personalities that lend themselves to this skill, naturally; those that stand out from the sidelines.

Being an effective, vocal goalkeeper is a combination of personality, experience, and game understanding – all of which take time to develop and grove. Patience is a virtue, they say, and coaches must show patience as they develop this area of goalkeeping.

Warm-Up

With all sports, a full warm-up is crucial. The warm-up allows you to become physically ready for match actions, and psychologically prepared for the occasion.

The warm-up should include more than just kicking endless balls at the goalkeeper as: a) this doesn't meet the holistic needs of match requirements and b) if the goalkeeper spends his time picking balls out of the net from a continuous shooting exercise, they will be fatigued and their confidence going into the game will be diminished.

Building more 'decision-based activities' into a goalkeeper's warm-up is something I strongly advocate. A goalkeeper should feel adequately prepared rather than what might be termed 'going through the motions'.

I've seen many different ideas fed into match warm-ups. When I was playing, I wanted a quick 15 to 20-minute warm-up: a few shots, a feel for the conditions taking crosses and through balls, then (finally) some distribution methods. Others want a 45 to 50-minute warm-up that includes shots from different angles and with different paces, alongside a selection of match scenarios.

If a player is fortunate enough to have a goalkeeping coach on match days, take guidance as to what the warm-up should include. Ultimately, the warm-up is designed to make a player *feel ready* for the match. If a player wants to include something to make them feel even more ready, they should ask the coach. In the same way, if there is an exercise that is felt *not to work*, then communication with the coach is needed.

Coaches should ask their goalkeepers to design a warm-up that they feel is good for them and which prepares them best. This is much easier for older goalkeepers as they understand their game's needs better; for younger ages, a more constructed and coach-led approach would be more effective, although they would still need to be comfortable with this.

Little tips

- In the warm-up, serve balls with both feet – this way, the goalkeeper gets used to a variety of shots and through balls from both left and right feet (should apply in training too).
- Don't be worried about serving a few shots wide – this way, the goalkeeper can judge the goal area and differently-paced shots.
- Along with getting the goalkeeper used to general shots from different angles – as well as crossing, through balls and distribution methods – try doing an exercise where the goalkeeper has to make decisions and adopt different starting positions.

In reality, most young goalkeepers will not get a fully sufficient warm-up due to the fact that, outside the professional game, the presence of a goalkeeping coach on match days is rare.

Being physically prepared is very important, but being switched on psychologically, and fully ready to play, is an area that rarely gets as much attention as it should.

Warm-up examples – without a goalkeeping coach

Here are a few tips that you can do if you don't have a goalkeeping coach, or a designated coach/parent to help you warm up:

- Go for a walk across and around the whole pitch with a ball (not around the perimeter but the whole area) – this will allow you to see the state of the pitch. By bouncing the ball and having the ball at your feet, you can see the run, along with any uneven areas. Passing the ball in front of you can show you the speed of the pitch.
- Now do the same but pay extra attention to the penalty area (use the one you will warm up in; this can also be done before the second half starts). Stand in the six-yard box and rehearse playing out from the back, goal kicks, taking crosses and coming for through balls – do this without the ball. This will help with becoming used to the goalkeeper movements on this particular pitch.
- With a ball, perform familiarity exercises like moving the ball around your body and passing the ball between each arm.

If you can use a substitute player, then do the following

- Get the goalkeeper to stand in the centre of the goal, about three yards out, and get the substitute player (who's about 12 yards out) to pass the ball aiming past either post at a steady pace. The keeper should take a touch and pass the ball back to them. After six passes, each side changes the activity to moving your hands into line with the ball and rolling it back. Change the angle by doing this from the left and the right.

All in all, a warm-up is very much an individual conquest for a goalkeeper. Rather than being in a warm-up where a matchday squad of players need to be catered for, the goalkeeper can effectively design their own warm-up and can put real thought into what gets their juices flowing before a game.

World Wide Web

The internet and the inexorable rise of social media have opened up a huge number of opportunities for the goalkeeping world. These include websites, podcasts, e-books, session sharing on Twitter, YouTube videos of sessions/matches, and players showcasing their abilities through LinkedIn and WhatsApp coaching groups.

Information can be shared easily between people, and this has enabled historically high levels of collaboration between like-minded personnel; most readers would no doubt have used some of these platforms over recent years.

Content ignites debate and discussion over all things goalkeeping – from styles to goals analysis right through to what glove brand is best.

The ability for coaches to showcase their sessions and what they're working on is valuable for the enhancement of practice design ideas, tactical approaches, means of analysis, and for developing positional understanding.

Players can post their clips online to promote their performances and build their fanbases, which brings in various commercial opportunities – promoting gloves and equipment brands being the most common.

Also, for players on the lookout for a new club, they can use these platforms to connect with clubs to showcase themselves and potentially gain a trial or a contract.

The opportunities that have been generated are vast, but during this technological age, I reckon we've only just scratched the surface.

Task

Visit social media and make a note of your favourite five pieces of goalkeeping-related content. This could be from any platform, a podcast or video – then share these five pieces with someone in your network or maybe a colleague.

This sharing of information and discussion will fuel debate and pass on knowledge.

Xavi

Xavi? The Spanish midfielder? Why does he have his own entry?! Well, if all keepers could be as comfortable on the ball as Xavi Hernandez, the ex-Spain and Barcelona playmaker, imagine how much of a weapon they would be!

Including the goalkeepers in possession practices such as Rondos and transfer games allow them to become more comfortable on the ball, play under pressure, and able to play penetrative passes.

The keeper, after all, is just a player with gloves on...

X-Factor

Having an X-Factor as a goalkeeper, or a unique selling point (USP), is fundamental to standing out from the crowd. From a goalkeeping perspective, this might take the form of being aerially dominant, an outstanding distributor, amazing speed and agility around the goal, an effective sweeper-keeper, calm and collected in all situations and never flustered, or having physical prowess, such as a 6ft 5in + frame.

This X-Factor may take a while to find and then to train. A player's personality can reflect what type of personality and physique they have – but whatever this X-Factor might be, the quicker it's found, the better!

Yardstick

A yardstick, in common usage, means using someone or something as a standard for comparison.

Comparing yourself to others, as a player, has its pros and cons, and whilst building your game around similar traits to others is useful, finding your own style as a goalkeeper can't be underestimated.

Nonetheless, if you say, 'I want to play like David de Gea' or 'I want to be like Ann-Katrin Berger', from a broad performance characteristic angle, this makes sense. The attributes they possess make them among the best keepers in the world, and having role models has been found to be highly constructive.

On a more local scale, comparing yourself to your peers or someone in a similar place is a waste of time. What someone can do that you can't (or can't yet) can be because of factors such as maturation, genetics, and environment.

An example would be two goalkeepers in the same team (or age bracket), where one can kick the ball a lot further than the other, and the keeper with the shorter range gets down on themselves due to this fact. There may well be reasons for this, as stated above, so using this player as a yardstick for yourself is not beneficial.

Looking at what *YOU* can get better and find ways to do this is what matters.

The yardstick of how you're doing and what you hope to achieve should be towards one person, *and that's yourself.*

Yashin, Lev

Lev Yashin was a Soviet professional footballer regarded by many as the greatest goalkeeper in the history of the sport. He was known for his athleticism, positioning, stature, bravery, imposing presence in goal, and acrobatic reflex saves.

Yashin earned his iconic status by revolutionising the goalkeeping position and imposing his authority on the entire defence. A vocal presence in goal, he shouted orders at his defenders, came off his line to intercept crosses and ran out to meet onrushing attackers. This was all done at a time when goalkeepers spent the 90 minutes just standing in the goal, waiting to be called into action. His performances made an indelible impression on a global football audience at the 1958 World Cup, the first to be broadcast internationally. Dressed head to toe in black, and earning his nickname the 'Black Spider', Lev Yashin was the first superstar keeper.

In 1994, FIFA established the "Lev Yashin Award" for the best goalkeeper at the World Cup finals and in 2020 Yashin was named in the FIFA Ballon d'Or Dream Team, the greatest all-time XI.

Zero Goals

The best way to finish the book! 'Clean-sheet', 'Shutout', 'Denied'… all of these mean the same thing – no goals conceded. The holy grail for any goalkeeper at all levels.

An important approach to take is that a keeper shouldn't judge their performances on the number of clean sheets they achieve or the number of goals they concede. Many factors go into achieving this aim, including the competence of defenders, the opposition played against, and refereeing decisions. If a defender decides to take out an attacker and give away a penalty, and they score the resulting penalty, then this is a harsh way to give up the clean sheet!

Whether a clean sheet has been achieved or not shouldn't define a goalkeeper's overall rating. There are many better ways to assess performance. These might include defined match objectives or a spotlight on a keeper's focus area (e.g., passing success).

Many young keepers see success as not conceding goals, and base how they've done on how many goals they've let in. This is dangerous as it's an easy out, due to the objective nature of the score (the score is the score, after all!). What's more valuable is looking at performance more scientifically and reviewing it in depth.

Check out all Andy's goalkeeping books,
plus our other coaching books at:

www.BennionKearny.com/soccer

www.ingramcontent.com/pod-product-compliance
Lightning Source LLC
LaVergne TN
LVHW041300080426
835510LV00009B/814